Walkers', Cyclists' and Horse Riders'

LightFoot Guide to the Three Saint's Way

Mont St Michel to Saint Jean d'Angely
Along the Plantagenet Way
547 Kilometres

Copyright © 2008/2012 Pilgrimage Publications All rights reserved.
ISBN: 978-2-917183-05-2
Revised:2012

Also by Babette Gallard and Paul Chinn
Riding the Milky Way - Long Riders' Press 2006
Riding the Roman Way - Pilgrimage Publications 2007
LightFoot Guides to the via Francigena 2008/9/10/12
LightFoot Guide to the via Domitia 2011
Reflections - A Pictorial Journey Along the via Francigena, 2008
LightFoot Guide to the The Three Saints' Way - Winchester to Mont St Michel, 2008
Reflections- A Pictorial Journey Along the Three Saint's Way, 2009
YOUR CAMINO - a Guide to Practical Preparation for a Pilgrimage, 2011

The authors have done their best to ensure the accuracy and currency of the information in this LightFoot Guide, however they can accept no responsibility for any loss, injury or inconvenience sustained by any traveller as a result of information contained in the guide. Changes will inevitably occur within the lifespan of this edition and the authors welcome notification of such changes and any other feedback that will enable them to enhance the quality of the guide.

Pilgrimage Publications is a not-for-profit organisation dedicated to the identification and mapping of pilgrim routes all over the world, regardless of religion or belief. Any revenue derived from the sale of guides or related activities is used further to enhance the service and support provided to pilgrims.

Pilgrimage Publications has been created by Paul Chinn and Babette Gallard, two people who have covered many hundreds of pilgrim kilometres. The ethos of their operation is based on four 4 key aims:
1. To enable walkers, cyclists and riders to follow pilgrim routes all over the world.
2. To ensure Pilgrimage Publications guides are as current as possible, using pilgrim feedback as a major source of information.
3. To produce LightFoot Guides or any other materials using only the most environmentally friendly option currently available.
4. To promote eco-friendly travel.

Tracing Yesterday Using Today's Technology

LightFoot Guides are designed to enable everyone to meet his/her personal goals and enjoy the best, whilst avoiding the worst, of following ancient pilgrimage routes. Written for Walkers, Cyclists and Horse Riders, every section of this LightFoot guide provides specific information for each group.

LightFoot Guides provide metre-by-metre instructions based on GPS co-ordinates, supported by Online Updates and are produced using the Print On Demand method - the most environmentally friendly option currently available.

The authors would also like to emphasise that they have made great efforts to use only public footpaths and to respect private property. Historically, pilgrims may not have been so severely restricted by ownership rights and the pressures of expanding populations, but unfortunately this is no longer the case. Today, even the most free-spirited traveller must adhere to commonly accepted routes. Failure to do so will only antagonise local residents, encourage the closure of routes - some examples of which have already been encountered - and selfishly detract from the experience of the pilgrims following on behind.

Revised editions of this guide will be published each year, but everyone is advised to refer to the relevant update page on the Pilgrimage Publications website, because changes will be immediately listed here when they are received.

ACKNOWLEDGEMENTS
Pilgrimage Publications has been developed and supported by more people than could possibly be listed here, but the authors would particulary like to thank the following individuals for their contribution to this first LightFoot Guide to the Three Saint's Way:
Barbara Edgar, for her thorough, sometimes painful (for the authors) proof-reading.
Marion Marples, Confraternity of St James, for her expert input and for highlighting the need for this guide.
Jeffrey Salter, for his stunning and highly professional photographs of Mont St Michel.

SECTION	CONTENTS	PAGE
	About Pilgrimages and Pilgrims	4
	About the Plantagenet's Way	5
	About Your LightFoot Guide	6
	About Map Symbols	7
	About Travel	8
	About the Basics in France	11
	About Transporting Horses	12
	About Transporting Dogs	13
	About Useful Links and Reading	14
	About General French Vocabulary	15
	About Cycling / Equine French Vocabulary	16
Section One	Mont St Michel to St James	18
Section Two	St James to Montours	22
Section Three	Montours to Fougéres	26
Section Four	Fougéres to Chatillon-en-Vendelais	31
Section Five	Chatillon-en-Vendelais to Vitré	35
Section Six	Vitré to Guerche-de-Bretagne	40
Section Seven	Guerche-de-Bretagne to Pouancé	44
Section Eight	Pouancé to Segré	49
Section Nine	Segré to Lion d'Angers	57
Section Ten	Lion d'Angers to Angers	63
Section Eleven	Angers to Brissac-Quincé	71
Section Twelve	Brissac-Quincé to Rochemenier	79
Section Thirteen	Rochemenier to Montreuil-Bellay	84
Section Fourteen	Montreuil-Bellay to Thouars	90
Section Fifteen	Thouars to Airvault	97
Section Sixteen	Airvault to Parthenay	106
Section Seventeen	Parthenay to Champdeniers-Saint-Denis	114
Section Eighteen	Champdeniers-Saint-Denis to Niort	120
Section Nineteen	Niort to Beauvoir-sur-Niort	128
Section Twenty	Beauvoir-sur-Niort to Aulnay	135
Section Twenty-one	Aulnay to St Jean d'Angely	142
	Religious Organisation Contact Information	150
	Map Reference Chart	152
	Pilgrim Record	155

The idea of sacred motion or travel runs deep in human religion, dating back to when early humans would climb hilltops to be closer to God or go to a specific spot to dance around in circles.

Spiritual talk is full of the language of travel : walking the walk, leaving behind, stepping forward and following God's paths on our spiritual journey of life.

Christian pilgrims have travelled across Europe since medieval times and for a variety of reasons. The majority would have been heading for three main sites of devotion, mostly on foot, covering anything up to 20 or 30 kilometres a day and usually carrying one of the three pilgrimage emblems: a scallop shell for Santiago de Compostela in Spain, keys for Saint Peter in Rome and a cross or palm leaf for Jerusalem. For some the motivation would have been entirely religious, but for many others it was far more basic and earthly - the sick hoping saintly relics would cure their bodily ills, criminals forced to take the long haul as a custodial sentence and the rest banking on enhanced pilgrim credibility and status when they got back home.

Today's Pilgrim

"*To set out on a pilgrimage is to throw down a challenge to everyday life.*"
Phil Cousineau - the Art of Pilgrimage

The pilgrimage is experiencing a renaissance. In 1986, just 2,491 pilgrims collected their Compostela certificate in Santiago, but by 2006 these figures had passed the 100,000 mark. Today's pilgrimage attracts people of all ages and beliefs, their primary common factor being the need to stand back from the daily pressures and take time to reflect on their lives and the lives of those around them. Most pilgrims choose to travel on foot, but others opt for bicycles, horses, cars or even public transport.

Today's pilgrims also travel for a variety of reasons other than the strictly devout, but ultimately, whatever the original motivation, everyone will find themselves changed by the experience, including the people living along the route who will profit from a cross-cultural exchange and of course the pilgrim trade. Travelling as a Pilgrim can only ever be at the speed your own body and mental attitude will allow, which may initially seem like a restriction. However, even the most cynical and reluctant newcomer will quickly realize that this is in fact a first step on the road to freedom. Clearly there will be days when you wonder why the hell you are there, but rest assured, this is only a temporary condition and you will find the answer in the people you meet and the memories you take away.

Road to the Stars

From the 9th century, pilgrims have followed the route of the sun to the west and at night they replaced this with a stream of stars, the Milky Way. The aim of their journey was to visit the tomb of St. James the Great, one of the twelve apostles of Christ, who tradition believes to be entombed in the cathedral of Santiago de Compostela. Many of those early pilgrims would have been making  their way to the four main starting points of the St James Way in France, which suggests that today there should be clearly identifiable routes. Of course the reality is that they chose a variety of roads, paths and sometimes open country to suit their personal requirements, and it is only in today's organized and prescribed environment that we look for the single Pilgrim route. The name, Three Saint's Way, has been created by the authors of your LightFoot guide and is based on the three saints associated with this pilgrimage: St Swithin, St Michael and St James. Far from being a single route, it is in fact a collection of intersecting routes, comprised of the Millenium Footpath Trail in England and the *Chemin Anglais* in France, which ultimately leads onto the Way of St James in St Jean d'Angely. This guide covers the second section of the route, starting in Mont St Michel on the *Chemin Anglais*, which takes pilgrims to St Jean d'Angely where the route intersects with the Way of St James starting from Paris.

 The name Plantagenet is derived from the common broom plant, known as "planta genista" in Latin. The House of Plantagenet, also called the House of Anjou, or the First Angevin dynasty, was originally a noble family from France, which ruled the county of Anjou. The name was first associated with Geoffrey of Anjou, father of King Henry II of England, either because he wore a sprig of broom in his bonnet, or because he planted broom to improve his hunting covers.

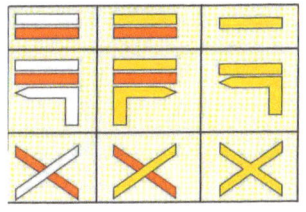 

Signs to Look Out For:
the paths you will be following are signposted by two organisations: the FFRP (Federation Française de la Randonnée Pedestre) and the Friends of the Chemin de St Jacques.

Pilgrim Record
A pilgrim's record was and still is used as proof of pilgrim status and to provide a pilgrimage log.

In France, most hotels, tourist offices and of course churches, will provide stamps for your pilgrim record.

Using Your Lightfoot Guide
This book traces the Three Saint's Way, from Mont St Michel to Saint Jean d'Angeley. In it you will find an introductory section followed by 21 chapters, each of which covers a segment of the route.

Each chapter contains:
* A route summary
* A cultural and historical overview of the region
* Detailed Instructions
* Map

Accommodation Listings:
Accommodation prices are based on one double room per night - accurate at the time of entry, but subject to change. For simplicity, the listing is divided into 3 price bands:

B1 0-20 ☐   B2 21-50 ☐   B3 51-70 ☐

In general there are no listings above 60☐ per night, unless nothing else is available in the area. Prices may or may not include breakfast and some establishments charge a tariff for dogs. The general rule for Religious hostels is that reservations must be made 24 hours ahead of arrival.

At the end of this section you will also find details of churches and religious organisations either in or near towns along the route.

Look out for the PR - Pilgrim Recommended - in front of listings
Layout
The entire distance has been divided into manageable sections of approximately 15 kilometres, but accommodation (where it exists) is listed for the entire length of the section so that is up to you and your body where you decide to stop.
Instructions
The entire route has been GPS traced (a total of 1300 waypoints and routing instructions) and logged using way point co-ordinates. On this basis, it should be possible to navigate the route using only the written instructions, though a map is provided for additional support and general orientation. Use of a compass is recommended.
Each instruction sheet provides:
*Detailed directions corresponding to GPS way point numbers on the map
*Verification Point - additional verification of current position
*Distance (in metres) between each way point
Each map provides:
*A north/south visual representation of the route with way point numbers
*Altitude Profile for the section (for accurate reading note scale for each Profile)
*Icons indicating places to stay, monuments etc. (see Map symbols)
*Relevant signs to look out for along the route
*Map reference number/s for the section

| Restaurant
| Café
| Accommodation
| Grocery
| Campsite
| Tourist Information Office
| Railway Station
| Equestrian Centre
| Monument
| Airfield
| Major church or other religious building
| Parish church
| Canal
| Railway
| River
| Motorway or major road
| Main road
| Minor road
| - on road
| - off road
| Alternate route - on road
| Alternate route - off road

About Map Symbols

Food, drink and a place to collapse at the end of the day

This route attracts only a fraction of the number of pilgrims found on the Way of St James from Paris and has the corresponding number of pilgrim hostels - very few. Similarly, do not expect to meet cohorts of pilgrims, this is an undeveloped route, which brings its own advantages, but it is an aspect everyone needs to be aware of before starting out. The **English section** - Winchester to Portsmouth (also known as the Millenium Footpath Trail) - is relatively short and through a well populated area, meaning you are unlikely to die of hunger or thirst on the way, though if you are looking for accommodation to break the section, then you are advised to book ahead. **The French section** is better than some areas in central France, but be aware that France has sold its soul to the car and hyper market, with the result that you will be lucky to find a café or shop in anything smaller than a town. And even if you do, you can bet your bottom Euro that it will be closed for lunch or *en vacances*. In short, the watch-word is assume the worst, carry food for the day, stop where you know you can replenish your supplies and always phone ahead to ensure that the place you have chosen to stay in still exists, is open and has a room available for the night you need it. But, having given you a bleak view of France, it is also important to stress that the French are extremely welcoming and a knock on the door of the local priest or *Mairie* will usually end in a solution. **Note:** the French are generally very accommodating with regard to dogs, though if you are continuing on into Spain, you will find the reception far less friendly.

Cyclists - To Road or Off-road

Quite simply if you are a Road Biker our route is not for you, though of course it is possible to follow an approximate version of the *Chemin Anglais* by using road maps. Off-road bikers can go just about anywhere a walker or horse can, but there are occasions when the pain/pleasure ratio makes other options preferable and sensible. We have ridden both horses and bikes the length of the route and know the disadvantages and pleasures of each, so it is with this experience in mind that we offer alternatives where we think it necessary. Of course ultimately these are only guidelines and everyone has to make their own choice. In terms of what kind of bikes you should use, clearly something fairly robust.

Horses and Riders - to Go or not to Go

Make no mistake, riding along the *Chemin Anglais* is going to be full of unexpected challenges. For people travelling without back-up, finding fodder and a place to stay will be the greatest challenge, but turning up in a village or town with a horse and a Don Quixote air can have the most amazing, invariably positive, outcomes. The route itself is possibly the easiest and most enjoyable long distance ride the authors have experienced to date. A great deal is off-road, through stunning countryside and with no real challenges. There are a number of equestrian establishments listed along the way, but essentially pilgrim riders must use their initiative and be prepared to ask for help. As for farriers and vets, they are also listed, but of course we cannot guarantee their competence or availability.

Signs Are Not Always What They Seem To Be

It is a feature of French roads that the responsibility for their maintenance can be transferred between state and commune. The most obvious change is in the number, which can be confusing for the uninitiated. Basically it is very simple. *Route Nationale* or 'N' roads can become minor roads, classed as 'D' roads, which means dropping the N, adding a D and then a number - for example the N32 is now the D1032.

Behaviour on the Road - preserve our heritage

Following pilgrim routes on foot, bicycle or horse is potentially the most eco-friendly form of travel possible. It can also benefit the local economy so that pilgrim tourists are always welcome, but this will only be the case if a few very simple rules are followed. Some sections of popular pilgrim routes are ruined by pilgrim detritus: plastic bottles, bags, tissues, sanitary towels, toilet paper ... an unsightly mess that is also a great deal more serious for the environment and wildlife. Everyone is responsible for the maintenance of these historic routes and should dispose of their rubbish in the appropriate way. Horse riders face an additional responsibility in this respect, because horses/donkeys can destroy turf and decimate gardens in seconds. Large piles of steaming, fly-clustered manure outside a restaurant are not good for trade and people do not like having metal shod hooves on their open-toed sandals. Whether you are walking, cycling or riding, please think about these points when you are travelling

Health and Safety

The most general and obvious health and safety tips apply to everyone; walker, cyclist or rider. This route should present no serious problems even to a beginner, provided you follow a few simple rules.

* Don't take unnecessary risks by tackling overly long or difficult routes.
* Know where you are or have a map and the ability to read it.
* On longer walks, be aware of "escape routes" in case you need to cut your walk short.
* Make sure you have plenty to eat and drink and are adequately dressed for the length of time you'll be out.
* Check the forecast before you set out and keep an eye on the sky. Rain, mist or fog and cold are the obvious hazards.
* The route recommended by this guide avoids roads wherever possible, but you will encounter some. In these situations, use the pavement if there is one and safe crossings wherever possible.

Walkers

Walking up hills increases the work load and energy cost considerably; even walking down again uses more energy than walking on the flat. Walking downhill can also make you sore if you're unaccustomed to it, because it uses muscles as shock absorbers. Plan rest days to allow your muscles and feet to recover. There is some controversy over how to treat blisters when they do occur. Some walkers prefer to burst the blister carefully and immediately apply a sterile dressing. Others argue this runs the risk of infection, and instead recommend gel-filled blister plasters. Either way, injuries and blisters are miserable and if serious enough can put an end to your plan, so avoidance is the best tactic.

Rucksack: The general principle should be to carry only what you need and no more. This route will not take you far away from civilization and on most days shops, hotels and hostels will be easily accessible, though riders with horses may have to plan further ahead. In all cases your rucksack should be large enough to take a tent and sleeping bag, if only as a fallback measure if things go awry.

Footwear: You will only need a pair of light walking boots, because you will not encounter any severe climbs (in France at least), but you should take a pair of comfortable sandals or trainers to give your feet a break at the end of the day.

Clothing: Waterproofs are a must, along with a fleece for the cooler evenings. Plan according to the time of year that you are travelling, but never rely on the weather. It will always do the unexpected.

Cyclists

The reality of long distance unsupported cycling trips is that you have to carry everything with you, and you have to wash clothes every night so Lycra is a good option. If you are thinking of cycling, you probably have your own bicycle already and providing it is a reasonable quality mountain bike, it will be adequate. Try to minimise the weight you are carrying. The more weight the greater the energy output required to carry it. There is a wide variety of racks available to support your panniers, but choose one of solid construction because it will take a lot of punishment. The mountings and securing nuts must be checked daily.

Injuries: The most common causes of cycling-related injuries are incorrect riding posture, such as putting too much weight on the hands and riding with straight elbows. Knee injury is generally due to overuse and occurs when a cyclist is doing too much, too fast. Once you've crested the hill, avoid the temptation to coast down the other side. Pedal a little bit to reduce the risk of lactic acid build-up in your leg muscles.

Horses and Riders

Don't even consider going on the via Francigena with your horse or donkey before you have ensured that:
* He/she is one hundred percent traffic proof
* He/she is familiar with crowds and generally noisy places
* He/she can be tethered for a full night
* He/she can deal with a variety of different feeds.

Equipment: The equipment you take will be governed by two factors: importance and weight - two priorities you must literally weigh up before leaving. There are probably as many opinions as riders on the best equipment to be used, so we will not enter that particular minefield here. Use the tack that you know your horse can tolerate for extended distances without suffering from galls and use a saddle pad that will distribute the weight as much as possible. Be sure to test your equipment before you leave. Despite all of your best endeavours items will be lost, stolen or worn out by the time you return home, so be sure that what you take you will be happy to lose. If you want to use a pack pony, consult the professionals and make sure you test your gear and your pony thoroughly before you go. Don't carry a huge veterinary kit. A can of antiseptic spray, an anti-inflammatory gel or something similar, and (if you are allowed to) a course of antibiotics, is ample. You can find vets and chemists along the route without any difficulty.

Absolutely Indispensable:
* Canvas water buckets
* Plastic gloves and plastic bags to pick up the inevitable equine accident. Horse riders have as much responsibility for the behaviour of their horses as do dog owners for their dogs.
* We recommend leather chaps, a waterproof cape and a broad brimmed hat.

So there you have it, the few words of wisdom we have to offer. Pilgrim feedback is fundamental for the accurate maintenance of the information in this guide, so please let us know where the route has changed, our information is incorrect or you can add to what we have. And remember, you are not doing this for us, but for all the pilgrims who will follow in your footsteps.

Currency: Euro. Standard banking Hours: Monday-Friday 09.30-12.00 and 14.00-16.00. Closed on Sundays and usually Monday, with half day opening on Saturday morning

Post Offices (La Poste): Standard opening hours Mon - Fri - 09.30-12.00 and 14.00-17.00. Half day opening on Saturday morning.

You can make **domestic and international phone calls** from any **public telephone box** and can receive calls where there is a new logo of a ringing bell.

Emergencies - 112 will give you access to the following services: Fire, Police, Ambulance, Coastguard, Mountain rescue or Cave rescue. This is free and can be dialled from any telephone (including mobile phones).

Basic Business Hours - 08.00-12.00 and 14.00-18.00. Almost everything in France - shops, museums, tourist offices etc. - closes for two hours at midday. Food shops often don't reopen until half way through the afternoon, but close at 19.30 or 20.00. The standard closing days are Sunday and Monday in small towns, but you will find that many large supermarkets are now staying open throughout the day.

All EU citizens are eligible for free health care if they have the correct documentation. The UK's NHS care includes free visits to the local doctor, and paying a standard charge for prescriptions and dental treatment.

In France, the best way to eat breakfast is in a bar or café, at a fraction of the cost charged by most hotels. Expect a croissant or some bread with coffee or hot chocolate. At lunchtime and sometimes in the evenings you'll find most cafés and restaurants offering a *plat du jour*, which is by far the cheapest alternative if you don't fancy cooking yourself.

Internet Cafés - France is generally well-served with internet cafés, though finding a reliable directory for a fully comprehensive list has not been easy. Nevertheless, most Tourist Offices will provide access at 0.50◻ per 15 mins, as do the public libraries.

In country areas, in addition to standard hotels, you will come across **chambre d'hôtes** and **ferme auberge**, bed and breakfast accommodation in someone's house or farm. These are rarely an especially cheap option, usually costing the equivalent of a two star hotel.

Youth hostels (*auberges de jeunesse*) are great for travellers on a budget. They are often beautifully sited and they allow you to cut costs by preparing your own food in their kitchens or eating in cheap canteens. The majority will require that you are a member of the International Youth Hostel Federation.
Gîtes d'étape are basic but do not require membership and provide bunk beds with primitive kitchen and washing facilities at a reasonable price.

Campsites in France are nearly always clean and have plenty of hot water. On the coast there are superior categories of campsite where you will pay prices similar to those of a hotel for the facilities -bars, restaurants and usually elaborate swimming pools too. For horses, it is useful to know that campsite owners often allow horses to be tethered at the edge of the site.

Horses

If you are starting out from the UK with your horse you will need the following:

1. Export licence
Licence required to take your horse or pony out of the UK. The ferry company will ask for this at the port when you arrive to board the ferry. You can apply for this yourself from DEFRA (Department for Environment, Food and Rural Affairs), include the proof of value for ponies.

2. TRACES document

You can apply to DEFRA yourself or get your vet to apply for the health certificate for the country to which your horse is travelling. The certificate will be sent directly to your vet and you will need to make an appointment with him or her for the horse to be inspected no more than 48 hours before it leaves the UK. The ferry company will ask to see this at the port but will return it to you. You will need this in your destination country. You will need a health certificate to be issued and signed in your destination country to be able to return to the UK (not applicable for France or Ireland).

3. Route Plan
A form which you partially complete and then send off with your application for a health certificate. DEFRA will stamp the first section and send it back with the health certificate for you to complete during the journey. Do not allow any official to keep this en route. You must take this home and keep it for 6 months in case DEFRA want to inspect it.

For all initial export queries go to:
International Animal Health Division
Service Delivery Unit
Ceres House
2 Searby Road
Lincoln, LN2 4DT
Tel: 01522 563132
Fax: 01522 545014
Email: lincoln.iahsdu@animalhealth.gsi.gov.uk

For DEFRA: http://www.defra.gov.uk/

For more general information and assistance:
 http://www.gettingoutofhere.co.uk/horses.html

Dogs Travelling under the Pet Travel Scheme (PETS) - eligible in all EU countries

Dogs can enter the UK under PETS as long as they meet the rules, but they must not have been outside any of the EU or non-EU listed countries in the 6 calendar months before travelling to the UK.
Dogs that are resident in either the United Kingdom or one of the other qualifying countries can enter or re-enter the UK without quarantine provided they meet the rules of the Scheme.

For list of countries go to:
www.defra.gov.uk/animalh/quarantine/pets/procedures/support-info/other.htm

Animals from unlisted countries must spend 6 months in quarantine on arrival in the UK.
There are no requirements for pets travelling directly between the UK and the Republic of Ireland.
PETS procedures can be carried out in any of the listed qualified countries.

The six month rule for entry or re-entry to the UK
Your dog or cat may not enter the UK under PETS until six calendar months have passed from the date that your vet took the blood sample which led to a satisfactory test result (see below). Once the vet has issued the PETS documentation and that six month period has passed, the PETS documentation is valid for your pet to enter the UK.

The procedures:
* Before any of the other procedures for PETS are carried out, your pet must be fitted with a microchip so that it can be properly identified.
* Have your pet vaccinated.
* After the microchip has been fitted your pet must be vaccinated against rabies. There is no exemption to this requirement, even if your pet has a current rabies vaccination.
* Arrange a blood test
* After your pet has been vaccinated, it must be blood tested to make sure that the vaccine has given it a satisfactory level of protection against rabies.
* Get PETS documentation.

For animals being prepared in an EU country, you should get an EU pet passport. If you are preparing your animal in a non-EU listed country you will need to obtain an official third country veterinary certificate although note that Gibraltar, Norway, San Marino and Switzerland are also issuing passports. Before your pet re-enters the UK, it must be treated against ticks and a tapeworm not less than 24 hours and not more than 48 hours before it is checked in with an approved transport company for its journey into the UK.

Be warned - you must check with the ferry company whether you are allowed to take your dog outside a vehicle.

For More Information:
PETS Helpline on 0870 241 1710
www.defra.gov.uk/animalh/quarantine/pets/index.htm

About Useful Links and Reading

www.charente-maritime.org	Les Chemins de Saint-Jacques de Compostelle en Charente-Maritime. Obtainable from: Conseil Général de la Charente-Maritim, 85 Boulevard de la République 17076 La Rochelle Cedex 9 Tel: 0033 (0)5 46 31 70 00
www.PilgrimsTales.com	Pilgrim Tales, passionate about inspiring others with the possibility of discovery, understanding and peace through travel
www.theexpeditioner.com	The Expeditioner, travel-themed webzine.
www.csj.org.uk	Confraternity of St James providing a wealth of information about the many pilgrim routes to Santiago de Compostela in Spain as well as general guidance and advice to pilgrims.
www.stjamesirl.com	IRISH SOCIETY OF THE FRIENDS OF ST JAMES The site of the Irish equivalent to the CSJ.
www.scottishwalkingsticks.com/	A very brief example of how to make a stick by Derek Farrar.
www.thestickman.co.uk/	A commercial site by Keith Pickering but good for purchasing DIY stick-making supplies.
www.manche-tourisme.com/medianet-uk.htm	Manche, France Tourist Site
http://visitnormandy.org/Normandy.nsf/Visit/Meteo.htm	Weather Forecast Normandy
www.fuaj.org	French Youth Hostel Association
www.thelongridersguild.com/	Information resource for long riders
www.ecf.com/	EuroVelo, European cycle route network
http://uk.franceguide.com/	French Tourist Office main site
http://www.couchsurfing.com/	CouchSurfing is a worldwide network for making connections between travelers and the local communities they visit.

Further Reading

The Art of Pilgrimage	Phil Cousineau
The Pilgrim's France- a Travel Guide to the Saints	James & Colleen Heater
Have Saddle Will Travel	Don West
The Essential Walker's Journal	Leslie Sansone
Pilgrim Tales: On and Off the Road to Santiago	Nancy Frey

ENGLISH	FRENCH	ENGLISH	FRENCH
Sunday	dimanche	one	un
Monday	lundi	two	deux
Tuesday	mardi	three	trois
Wednesday	mercredi	four	quatre
Thursday	jeudi	five	cinq
Friday	vendredi	six	six
Saturday	samedi	seven	sept
January	janvier	eight	huit
February	février	nine	neuf
March	mars	ten	dix
April	avril	eleven	onze
May	mai	twelve	douze
June	juin	thirteen	treize
July	juillet	fourteen	quatorze
August	août	fifteen	quinze
September	septembre	sixteen	seize
October	octobre	seventeen	dix-sept
November	novembre	eighteen	dix-huit
December	décembre	nineteen	dix-neuf
today	aujourd'hui	twenty	vingt
yesterday	hier	thirty	trente
tomorrow	demain	forty	quarante
in the morning	le matin	fifty	cinquante
in the afternoon	l'après-midi	sixty	soixante
in the evening	le soir	seventy	soixante-dix
now	maintenant	seventy-five	soixante-quinze
later	plus tard	eighty	quatre-vingt
at midday	à midi	ninety	quatre-vingt-dix
at one o'clock	à une heure	one hundred	cent
bus	autobus, bus, car	on the other side of	à l'autre côte de
bus stop	arrêt	on the corner of	à l'angle de
bus station	gare routière	next to	à côte de
car	voiture	behind	derrière
train station	gare	in front of	devant
what time does it arrive/leave?	il arrive/part à quelle heure?	before	avant
how many kilometres	combien de kilomètres?	after	aprés
how many hours	combien d'heures?	under	sous
on foot	à pied	to cross	traverser
the road to	la route à	where?	ou?
near	prés/pas loin	when?	quand?
far	loin	how many/much?	combien?
left	à gauche	why?	pourquoi?
right	à droite	at what time?	a quelle heure?
straight on	tout droit	a room for one/two person/people	une chambre pour une/deux personnes

About General French Vocabulary

Cycling

ENGLISH	FRENCH	ENGLISH	FRENCH
to adjust	ajuster	to lower	baisser
axle	l'axe	mudguard	le garde-boue
ball bearing	le roulement à billes	pannier	le panier
battery	la pile	pedal	la pédale
bent	tordu	pump	la pompe
bicycle	le vélo	puncture	la crevaison
brake cable	le câble	to raise	relever
brakes	les freins	to repair	réparer
broken	cassé	saddle	la selle
bulb	l'ampoule	to screw	visser
chain	la chaine	spanner	la clef
to deflate	dégonfler	spoke	le rayon
frame	le cadre	to straighten	redresser
gears	les vitesses	stuck	coincé
grease	la graisse	tight	serré
handlebars	le guidon	toe clips	les cale-pieds
to inflate	gonfler	tyre	pneu
inner tube	la chambre à air	wheel	la roue

Equine

ENGLISH	FRENCH	ENGLISH	FRENCH
stud (to put in horse shoe)	un crampon	stirrup	etrier
mane	la crinière	saddle pad	tapis de selle
tail	la queue	brush	brosse
horse	cheval	hoof-picks	cure-pieds
mare	jument	horse shoe	fer
foal	poulain	helmet	bombe
gelding	hongre	hat	chapeau
stallion	entier / etalon	gloves	gants
head	tête	boots	bottes
eyes	yeux	walk	pas
ears	oreilles	trot	trot
nostril	naseau	canter	galop
withers	garrot	saddle	selle
croup (rear)	croupe	girth	sangle
neck	encolure	bridle	bride
to shorten	raccourcir	rope	longe
legs	jambes	to unsaddle	desseller
hoof	sabot	to girth	sangler
tack	harnachement (général)	to loosen the girth	dessangler
lame	boiter		

Pilgrims are poets who create by taking journeys
(Richard R. Niebuhr)

Le Mont Saint Michel to Saint James 22.2km

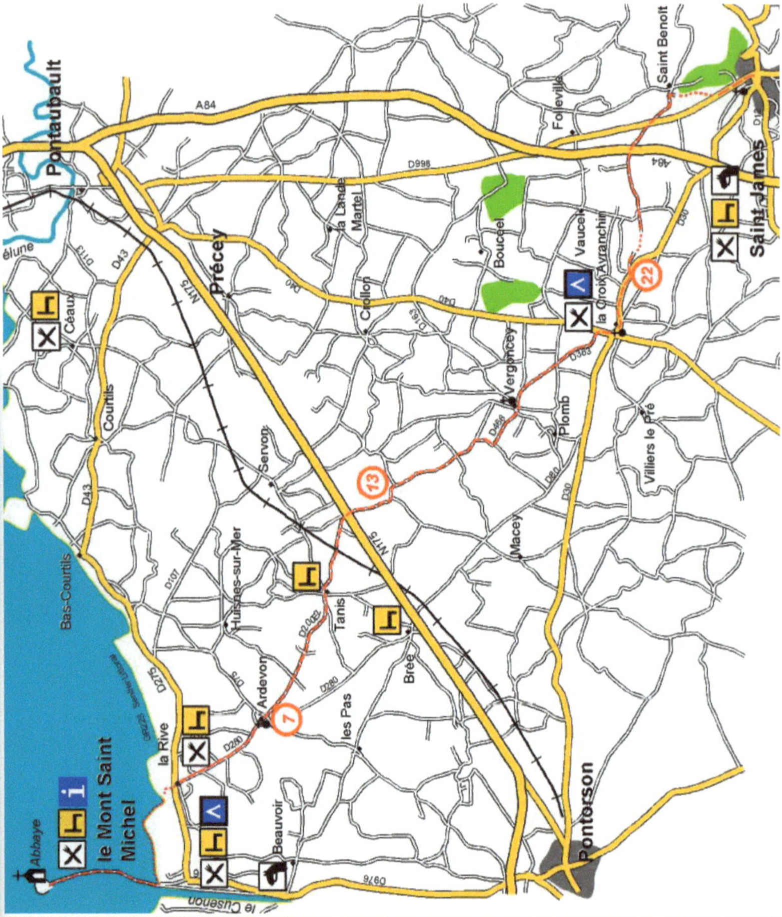

Route Summary: after leaving the coast the section is largely undertaken on quiet tarmac roads only briefly intersecting with more major roads

Way Point	Distance	Directions	Verification Point	Compass
1		From the entrance to le Mont Saint Michel, beside the Office du Tourisme, take the causeway towards the mainland	Continue with sheep pasture on the left	S
2	1900	At the end of the sheep pasture and before reaching the first building fork left onto track, not going through the gate and keeping line of fencing immediately on the right	Saint Jacques sign	E
3	1200	Bear right keeping fence to right all the way	GR signs	SE
4	400	Go through gate and turn left with fence on left and then sharp right along a track, again with fence on left		SE
5	300	Coming off track continue straight ahead direction Ardevon on D280	Pass Auberge de la Baie on the left	SE
6	1900	In the village of Ardevon continue straight ahead direction Tanis	Saint Jacques sign and church on right	SE
7	200	At the crossroads go straight ahead direction Tanis on D200	Crucifix on right	SE
8	1500	Continue straight ahead	Sign for route de la Baie	E
9	900	At crossroads go straight ahead direction Servon, on D200	rue de Miquelot	E
10	170	In Tanis, fork right onto rue des Landes direction la Dodemanerie	Saint Jacques sign	E
11	1300	Turn right onto rue de la Gare	Leaving rue des Landes	SE
12	150	Cross straight over main road, N175, direction Macey, on D200	St Jacques sign and rue de Noyant	S
13	800	Bear left direction Vergoncey		SE
14	1500	At crossroads go straight ahead direction Vergoncey	Saint Jacques sign	SE
15	400	Take right fork	Pass Dimanche on the right	S
16	300	Turn left on minor road	Saint Jacques sign	SE
17	800	At crossroad in the centre of Vergoncey continue straight ahead	Church on left	E

Le Mont Saint Michel to Saint James 22.2km

Way Point	Distance	Directions	Verification Point	Compass
18	50	Continue straight ahead direction la Croix Avranchin on D363	Church on left boulangerie on right	SE
19	1000	At crossroads continue straight ahead	Pass sign for la Masure	SE
20	1100	At crossroads turn right on D40, direction Antrain	Saint Jacques sign	S
21	170	At crossroads in la Croix Avranchin, turn left direction St James on D30	Bar on the right at the junction	E
22	1100	Turn left off the main road direction St Benoît on D363	Saint Jacques sign	E
23	2200	Continue straight over the road bridge	Autoroute A84	SE
24	700	Turn right on D998		SE
25	60	Turn left direction St Benoît on D363		SE
26	500	Turn right in centre of St Benoît, direction le Grand Moulin	St Jacques sign and church on right	S
27	300	Take left fork on track going between two large stones		S
28	500	Track comes out onto a minor road turn right towards the major road		SW
29	60	Turn left onto the major road into the town of Saint James, D998	Saint Jacques sign	SE
30	700	Arrive in the centre of Saint James at the crossroads with rue Patton, D30		

Le Mont Saint Michel to Saint James 22.2km

Accommodation	Price	Opening	Animals
La Rive, N° 7 La Rive 50170 ARDEVON Tel: 0033 (0)2 33 60 80 30 Mobile: 0033 (0)6 87 29 64 63	B1	All Year	🐴
La Jacotière 50170 ARDEVON Tel: 0033 (0)2 33 60 22 94 jacotiere@bedbreak.com www.bedbreak.com/lajacotiere	B3	All Year	🐴
11 Rue de la Saint Côme 50170 TANIS Tel: 0033 (0)2 33 60 14 89	B2	All Year	🐴
Mme DESGRANGES, Brée en Tanis 50170 TANIS Tel: 0033 (0)2 33 48 18 26	B2	All Year	🐴
110 Rue De La Liberation 50240 SAINT JAMES Tel: 0033 (0)2 33 58 90 25 petit-illyria@wanadoo.fr www.petit-illyria.eu.com	B2	All Year	❌
Tiffaine François et Catherine, La Gautrais 50240 SAINT JAMES Tel: 0033 (0)2 33 48 31 86	B2	All Year	🐴
Camping	Price	Opening	Animals
Du Mont Saint Michel, La caserne 50170 ARDEVON Tel: 0033 (0)2 33 60 22 10 www.camping-montsaintmichel.com	B1	23 June - 10 Sept	🐴
Camp Municipal Le Clos Ruault 50240 LA CROIX AVRANCHIN Tel: 0033 (0)2 33 48 24 40	B1	All Year	🐴

Equestrian Centre

Centre Equestre de La Dierge, enclos Dierge 50240 SAINT JAMES
Tel: 0033 (0)2 33 68 36 07 **Note:** Also gites d'Etape & Chambre d'hôte

Le Mont Saint Michel to Saint James 22.2km

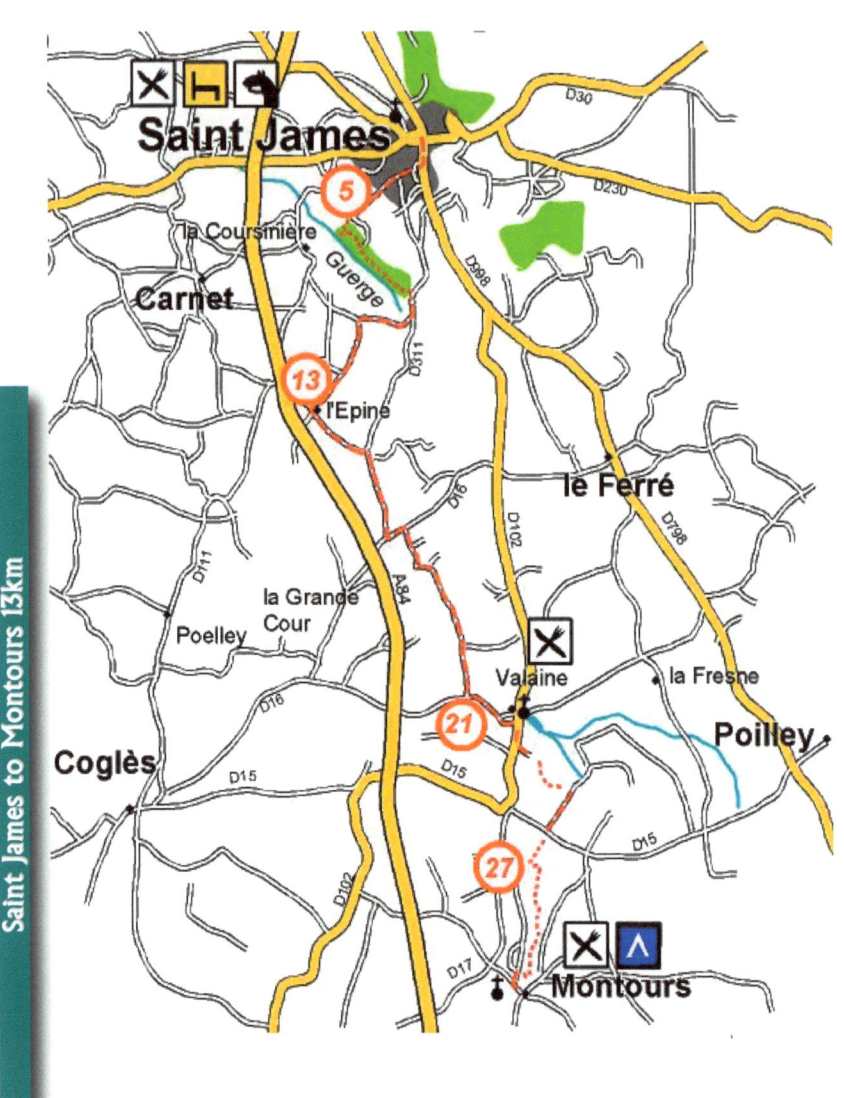

Route Summary: this segment is largely undertaken off-road on pleasant woodland and farm tracks. Shortly after Saint James the path passes through woodland with a short but steep climb in potentially slippery conditions. The path is passable for all groups, but may require cyclists to dismount for the climb

Way Point	Distance	Directions	Verification Point	Compass
1		From the crossroads with rue Patton, D30, continue along rue de la Libération		S
2	300	Bear right on rue Antoine Péry		S
3	120	Turn right to pass the sports ground on the right	Saint Jacques sign	SW
4	300	Continue straight ahead, direction Ferme de la Diérge		SW
5	600	Turn right off the road down a track	Saint Jacques sign and wooden pedestrian and cyclist signs	SW
6	200	Coming down the hill, turn sharp left back up the hill and towards some fields	Saint Jacques sign	SE
7	400	Bear right down the hill	Field on left and woods on right	S
8	60	Bear left into a swampy area - do not take the right hand track		SE
9	200	T-junction in tracks, turn left away from a small river		N
10	70	Turn sharp right	Saint Jacques sign and stone in middle of track	SE
11	500	Turn right, remaining on the grass track which runs parallel to the road	Saint Jacques sign	S
12	300	Turn right off grass track and onto road	Saint Jacques sign	SW
13	1700	Turn left direction Le Ferré	Saint Jacques sign	SE
14	600	Remain on road, do not take right turn to farmhouse		E
15	120	Turn right direction Le Ferré on D311	Saint Jacques sign	S
16	100	Continue straight ahead direction Coglès, on D311	Saint Jacques sign	S
17	900	Turn left with farm directly on left as you turn	Saint Jacques sign and sign for la Haie Bourel	NE
18	200	Fork right	Saint Jacques sign and sign listing a number of farms, including Le Pierre Chauvin	SE
19	1600	Turn right, la Pierre Chauvin	St Jacques sign	S
20	170	Continue straight ahead do not take the right turn towards the farm		S
21	400	T-junction, turn left	Crucifix on left	SE
22	600	At T-junction, turn right with village Valaine on left	Saint Jacques sign, Chapel ahead	S

Saint James to Montours 13km

Saint James to Montours 13km

Way Point	Distance	Directions	Verification Point	Compass
23	200	Turn left onto narrow track	Saint Jacques sign and house on left	SE
24	200	Turn right onto a farm track		SE
25	600	At T-junction with minor road turn right	Saint Jacques sign and sign for la Grande Brosse	SW
26	600	At junction with more major road, continue straight ahead on track	Crucifix on the left as you cross	SW
27	300	Turn left on farm track and join the circuit de Terre Rouge	Saint Jacques sign	E
28	110	Turn right onto narrow track before reaching the farm, le Haut Chemin	Saint Jacques sign	S
29	1100	Bear right shallow, flight of steps	Saint Jacques sign and water tower on right	S
30	140	Turn right avoiding track leading ahead		NW
31	100	Emerge from Chemin du Roc and turn left on the road	Large crucifix straight ahead	S
32	190	Turn left keeping the church to your right and arrive in the centre of Montours	Bar Tabac Au Bon Acueil on the left	

Accommodation - Hotel/B&B	Price	Opening	Animals
Devittori Rose-Marie, La Branche 35460 SAINT BRICE EN COGLES Tel: 0033 (0)2 99 97 77 95 **Note:** 4.55km from Montours	B1	All Year	🐴

Camping	Price	Opening	Animals
Aussant Pierre, Le Château Bonteville 35460 MONTOURS Tel: 0033 (0)2 99 95 16 60 **Note:** 3.2km from Montours	B1	All Year	🐴

Equestrian Centre

Les Ecuries d'Estran, lieu-dit Grand Champ 35460 SAINT BRICE EN COGLES
Mobile: 0033 (0)6 81 23 03 00 **Note:** 4.60km from Montours

Victor Hugo described **Fougères** as a "place where artists ought to flock like pilgrims" and Balzac described it as the "flower of Brittany". In mediaeval times it was a military post of great significance, and the 12th century moated castle, around which the town has developed over generations, still stands as a focal point and reminder of bygone days. With its 13 towers, the impressive fortress is one of the best conserved mediaeval castles in Europe. Fougères' major monument is a medieval stronghold built on top of a granite ledge, which was part of the ultimately unsuccessful defence system of the Duchy of Brittany against French aggression, and part of a tripartate with Vitré and Châteaubriant. A sizable section of the town walls survive stretching from the château in the lower town up the hill to surround the upper town. During the Middle Ages, salt was heavily taxed and was imported from the Breton regions to the rest of France. Fougeres was made a stronghold for "salt smugglers," who would creep along the wall of the city with confiscated salt, to sell in other regions. There is a communal garden in modern Fougeres that commemorates this interesting and little known fact. The church of Saint Sulpice, in the lower part of the town, was built in the mid 11th century and is a late Flamboyant Gothic building whose walls are highly and elaborately decorated with convoluted exterior displays of strange and savage gargoyles. Notre-Dame-de-Bonabry, built in 1893 in the Romanesque and Byzantine style was built to serve the owners and workers of shoe factories in the centre of which it was built.

Montours to Fougerèrs 18.7km

Useful Contacts
Tourist Offices
Office de Tourisme du Pays de Fougères, 2 r Nationale 35300 FOUGÈRES
Tel: 0033 (0)2 99 94 12 20   ot.fougeres@wanadoo.fr   www.ot-fougeres.fr/

Doctor
Bertrand Hervé, 3 r Albert Durand 35300 FOUGERES Tel: 0033 (0)2 99 94 57 57
Talbourdet Vincent, 34 quai Henri Chardon 50760 BARFLEUR
Tel: 0033 (0)2 33 43 24 00

Veterinary
Clinique véterinaire, 2 Bis pl République 35300 FOUGERES
Tel: 0033 (0)2 99 99 04 40

Farrier
Clossais Jonathan LE HAUT OURET 35133 LAIGNELET Mobile: 0033 (0)6 88 97 83 12

Montours to Fougèrers 18.7km

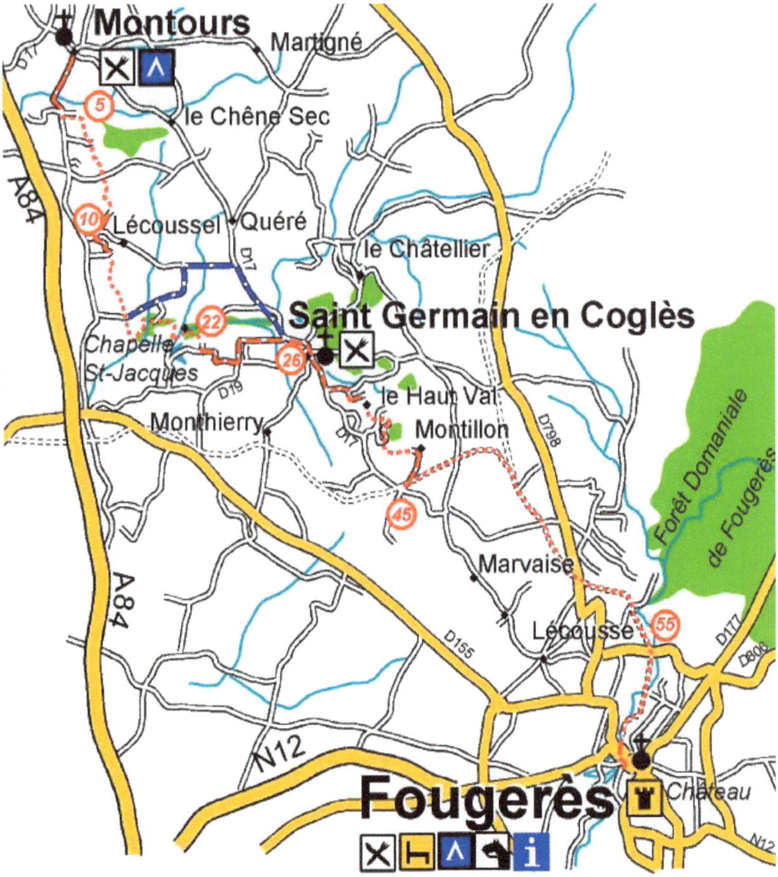

Route Summary: a pleasant section for all groups including an easy approach to the centre of Fougerès along the disused railway track. There is a short section of potentially wet and slippery pathway shortly before St Germain en Coglès – an alternate route is suggested for horse and bike riders.

Look out for: the brass St James scallop shells set into Fougéres pavements

Way Point	Distance	Directions	Verification Point	Compass
1		In centre of village of Montours beside the church, proceed down the hill keeping the church to your right		S
2	60	Continue straight ahead on rue Quincampoix		S
3	1000	Turn left, direction Rabines de Courtine	Mont St Michel, GR and St Jacques signs	E
4	200	Continue straight ahead on the road	Farm, la Morandais, to the left	E
5	90	Bear right on track	GR sign	S
6	400	At T- Junction turn left and then immediately right		SE
7	300	Bear left onto road	Montours on skyline to the left and behind	S
8	150	Continue straight ahead over a crossroads with a minor road	Signs for Rose des Vents	S
9	500	After double bend, take the right fork direction Rabines de Courtine and pass beside le Champ Juré	St Jacques sign	SW
10	300	At junction with a minor road turn right	Yellow right turn sign	SW
11	100	Turn left on track, the track immediately turns sharp left	Farm buildings to the right	SE
12	300	Continue straight ahead	Farmhouse, Lecoussel, and shed directly on left	SE
13	80	Bear left on track	Derelict farm on left	S
14	1000	Cross minor road to continue straight ahead. **Note:-** the path ahead can be wet and is also narrow with a short but steep climb. To avoid this turn left on the road and right at the T-junction. Turn right at the junction with the D17 to rejoin the main route at Waypoint #26	St Jacques sign and farm, Rochumaux, on left	S
15	300	Bear right leaving the road to enter the woods	House on left	SE
16	90	Turn left		NE
17	400	Follow track to the right up the hill		SE
18	140	Turn left onto road	Barn on left, house on right	NE

Montours to Fougèrers 18.7km

Montours to Fougèrers 18.7km

Way Point	Distance	Directions	Verification Point	Compass
19	160	Turn right onto track		SE
20	160	Continue straight ahead		S
21	200	Turn sharp left on track. **Note:-** pass beside Chapelle St Jacques	Keep lake to your right	E
22	500	Continue straight ahead on road	Pass beside the farm la Gapaillère	S
23	190	At T-junction turn left		E
24	600	At crossroads turn left	After double bend	N
25	300	Turn right on track	Pass beside la Bazillais	E
26	900	Bear right towards the centre of Saint Germain en Coglès	Ecole de St Jacques de Compostelle on left	S
27	300	In centre of Saint Germain en Coglès at roundabout turn left on rue de la Ecousse		SE
28	400	Turn left	Just beyond fire station	E
29	200	Bear right through hamlet	Impasse de la Haute Volerie	SE
30	50	Bear right remaining on road		SE
31	180	Turn left	St Jacques sign	E
32	160	Turn right on track	Derelict farm on left	S
33	300	At T-junction in track turn left	GR sign	E
34	140	At T-junction with road bear left	le Haut Val	E
35	90	At junction bear right	Do not enter le Bas Val	E
36	50	Continue to bear right away from le Bas Val	Farm on left	SE
37	70	Turn right	In front of house	SW
38	70	Straight ahead between houses	Le Rocher de Montillon	S
39	200	On crown of bend turn left on track		SE
40	300	Continue ahead with woods on the left		E
41	100	Continue straight ahead		E
42	160	Continue straight ahead on the road	Farmhouse, Montillon, on left	E

Way Point	Distance	Directions	Verification Point	Compass
43	110	Bear right down the hill	Mont St Michel signs on farm building	S
44	140	Continue straight ahead	Le Mont St Michel sign on telegraph pole	SW
45	300	Turn sharp left onto disused railway line converted to broad path/cycle track		NE
46	400	Continue along the cycle path crossing a farm track	GR sign	NE
47	300	Cross over minor road on track	St Jacques and GR sign on barriers	NE
48	300	Continue straight ahead through wooden barrier on same track		SE
49	1000	Cross minor road to continue on the cycle track	House on right and GR sign on wooden barrier	SE
50	500	Cross minor road to continue on cycle track	Les Tais	SE
51	400	Cross minor road to continue on cycle track	Farm house on left	SE
52	500	Cross major road to continue on the cycle track	House on right No.74	E
53	700	Cross minor road to continue on cycle track	House on left No. 71	SE
54	300	Cross minor road to continue on cycle track		SE
55	600	Cross straight over main road to continue on the cycle track	Wooden barriers	S
56	1300	Cross zebra crossing and continue ahead	Crossing rue du Guélandry	S
57	180	At the end of the gravel track turn right into the car park	Two tunnels straight ahead	SW
58	80	Having crossed the car park turn left up the hill direction château		SE

Montours to Fougêrers 18.7km

Way Point	Distance	Directions	Verification Point	Compass
59	110	Turn right on Allée du Manege	Direction Office de Tourisme	SW
60	50	At the T-junction at the top of the hill turn left, cross the road and proceed towards mini roundabout	Tour Montfromery on right as you turn	SE
61	40	Bear right at the mini roundabout		S
62	70	At the next traffic island bear right following the sign for Théâtre Victor Hugo	Keep between bollards	W
63	50	Having crossed the Place turn left onto rue Porte Roger		W
64	90	Arrive at the Office de Tourisme in Fougères	To the left of the theatre	

Montours to Fougères 18.7km

Accommodation	Price	Opening	Animals
Le Flaubert, 1 r Gustave Flaubert 35300 FOUGERES Tel: 0033 (0)2 99 99 00 43 hotel-leflaubert@ifrance.com http://hotel-leflaubert@ifrance.com	B1	All Year	🐴
Balzac Hôtel, 15 r Nationale 35300 FOUGÈRES Tel: 0033 (0)2 99 99 42 46 balzachotel@wanadoo.fr	B2	All Year	🐴
PR For Information for a variety of accommodation in and around Fougéres: Frederic Guérin, La Lanterne, 110 rue de la Pintérie, 35300 FOUGERES Tel: 0033 (0) 99 99 58 50 lalanternefougeres@orange.fr			
Hotel Gril Campanile, 28 rte Ernée 35300 FOUGÈRES Tel: 0033 (0)2 99 94 54 00 fougeres@campanile.fr	B2	All Year	🐴
Hôtel de Bretagne, 7 pl République 35300 FOUGÈRES Tel: 0033 (0)2 99 99 31 68 contact@hoteldebretagnefougeres.com	B2	All Year	🐴

Camping	Price	Opening	Animals
Aussant Pierre, Le Château Bonteville 35460 MONTOURS Tel: 0033 (0)2 99 95 16 00	B1	All Year	🐴
Camping Municipal de Paron, Paron 35300 FOUGERES Tel: 0033 (0)2 99 99 40 81 aft@francecom.com	B1	All Year	🐴

Equestrian Centre

Centre Hippique de Montaubert, rte Saint Malo Montaubert 35300 FOUGERES Tel: 0033 (0)2 99 99 03 52

Your route takes you through Ille-et-Vilaine. The department is named after its two main rivers, the Ille and the Vilaine, whose confluence is in Rennes, the capital of the region. Ille-et-Vilaine is moderately elevated above sea level with some hilly and densely forested areas, but also a dense network of small rivers.

Fougères to Châtillon-en-Vendelais 20km

Camping	Price	Opening	Animals
La Ferme du Faire à Cheval, La Regretté 35210 PARCE Tel: 0033 (0)2 99 97 64 71	B1	All Year	🐴
Camping Municipal, r Rouxières 35210 CHATILLON EN VENDELAIS Tel: 0033 (0)2 99 76 06 32	B1	All Year	🐴

Equestrian Centre

Le Haut Chemin Bigot, 35133 JAVENE Tel: 0033 (0)2 99 99 15 17

La Ferme du Faire à Cheval, La Regretté 35210 PARCE Tel: 0033 (0)2 99 97 64 71 **Note:** also includes a camping site

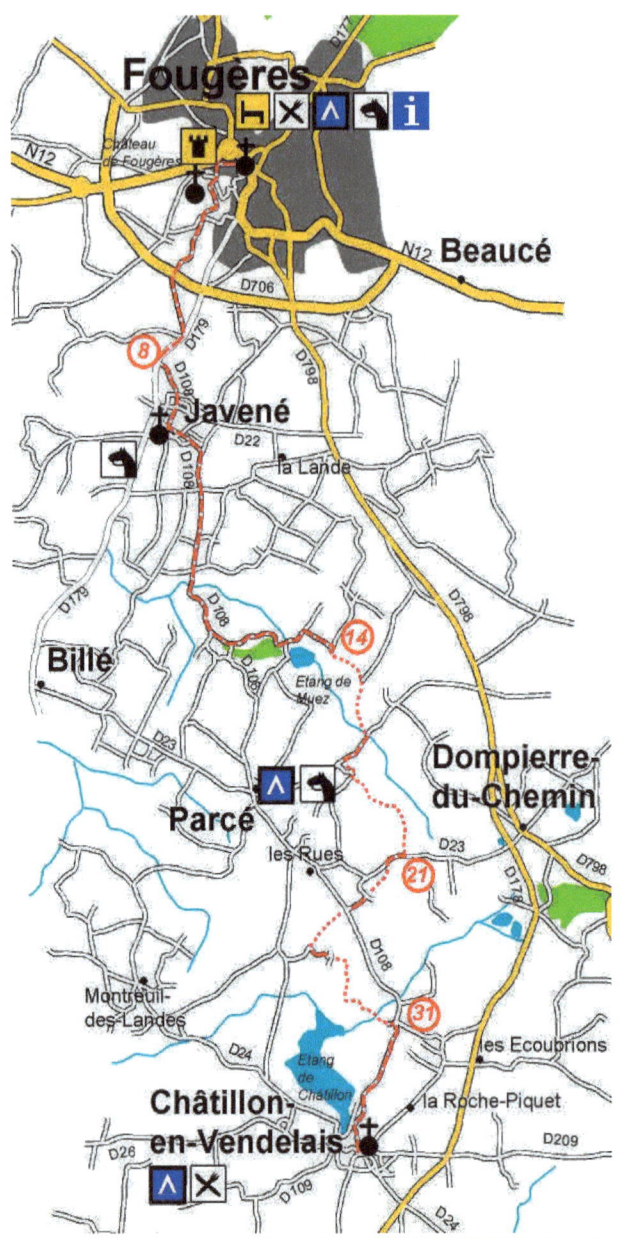

Fougères to Châtillon-en-Vendelais 20km

Route Summary: the route marking is very limited within the town or Fougères, but is excellent once the ring road is crossed. The route comprises generally quiet roads and farm tracks and makes for easy progress for all groups.

Way Point	Distance	Directions	Verification Point	Compass
1		Facing the entrance to the Office du Tourisme turn right and pass in front of the Théâtre Victor Hugo then turn left down the hill	Rue de la Pinterie	W
2	300	Fork left on rue de la Boutellier	Pass through Porte Notre Dame	SW
3	160	Turn left on rue de la Providence	Metal Mont Saint Michel sign set into pavement	SE
4	90	At the T-junction turn right and cross Place de Marchix		S
5	70	At the end of Place de Marchix continue straight ahead on rue de Savigny		S
6	500	At junction bear left direction Gibary on chemin de la République	Sign post for the Tour de Marches de Bretagne	S
7	1900	At T-junction with major road (D179) turn right		SW
8	600	Turn left to pass through Javené on the D108	St James sign	S
9	2200	At crossroads continue straight ahead, direction Parcé		S
10	2500	Turn left direction la Butte and la Rue	St James sign	E
11	800	At T-junction turn left keeping the lake on the right	St James sign	NE
12	400	Fork right towards farm in the valley	Lake to the right	SE
13	500	Turn right off the road and then again sharp right to pass around the left hand side of a farm building, direction la Gasnerais	St James sign	S
14	170	Turning left onto a grass track opposite the farm house	St James sign	SE
15	600	At junction turn right onto a minor road, with a farm yard directly on right – le Haut Monbelleux – and take the long straight farm track between fields	St James sign	S
16	800	At junction with a minor road turn right, a large factory building to the right	St James sign	SW
17	600	Turn left onto a minor road direction Les Bêches	St James sign	SE
18	200	Turn left onto a small track with a farm to the right as you turn	St James sign	SE

Fougères to Châtillon-en-Vendelais 20km

Way Point	Distance	Directions	Verification Point	Compass
19	400	Leave the grass track and continue straight ahead	St James sign	SE
20	500	Continue bearing right along the farm track	St James sign	S
21	700	T-junction turn right	St James sign	SW
22	300	Bear left direction la Champronnière	St James sign	S
23	200	Fork right onto a gravel track		SW
24	400	Continue straight ahead, avoid the turning towards the farm buildings		SW
25	300	Cross minor road to continue straight ahead on the grass track	St James sign	SW
26	800	Turn left towards a farm house – Mirtaux	St James sign	E
27	300	At crossroads continue straight ahead	St James sign	E
28	300	Bear right	St James sign	S
29	500	Continue bearing left	St James sign	E
30	300	At T-junction turn right down the hill and towards a group of farm buildings – la Loirie	St James sign	SE
31	600	At crossroads turn right with manoir on the right	St James sign	SW
32	1200	Continue straight ahead on the D108 keeping lake to the right	St James sign	S
33	400	Bear left into the car park and then at the end of the football pitch bear left again and continue towards the church spire. **Note:-** half way up the short climb towards the church you will see a St James sign for a path to the left. The path skirts the village to arrive at Way Point #3 on the following segment. If you chose to take the path be sure to turn right at the T-junction and sharp left at the large wodden cross	St James sign	S
34	500	Arrive in Châtillon-en-Vendelais on Place de l'Eglise		

Fougères to Châtillon-en-Vendelais 20km

Vitré is one of the best preserved medieval towns in Brittany. Its walls are not quite complete, but the clusters of medieval stone cottages have hardly changed since their construction. The towers of the castle have pointed slate-grey roofs in best fairy-tale fashion.

The site of Vitré was occupied in Gallo-Roman times and the name Vitré comes from the Gallo-Roman name "Victor" or "Victrix". The year 1000 marked the formal birth of Vitré, when the duke of Brittany, Geoffrey I, bestowed feudal powers upon Riwallon Le Vicaire, who was charged with keeping this strategic area as a buffer zone of the "Marches of Brittany". A small wooden motte-and-bailey castle, on a feudal mound, was built on the Sainte-Croix hill, but this was burned down on several occasions and was eventually bequeathed to the Benedictine monks of Marmoutiers. A stone castle was built in 1070 by Robert Ier on the current site and certain parts of the original stone castle still are visible today.

Notre-Dame church was reconstructed between 1440 and approximately 1580. Within its flamboyant gothic decor one can see Renaissance ornamental motifs and a "multiple-gabled" church which enables more light to enter.

In the 13th century, the castle was enlarged and equipped with robust towers and curtain walls. Since the 13th century, Vitré has joined together all of the elements of the traditional medieval city: a fortified castle, religious buildings, churches, colleges, and suburbs to become a truly fascinating and pleasant town in which to spend time.

Châtillon-en-Vendelais to Vitré 16.4km

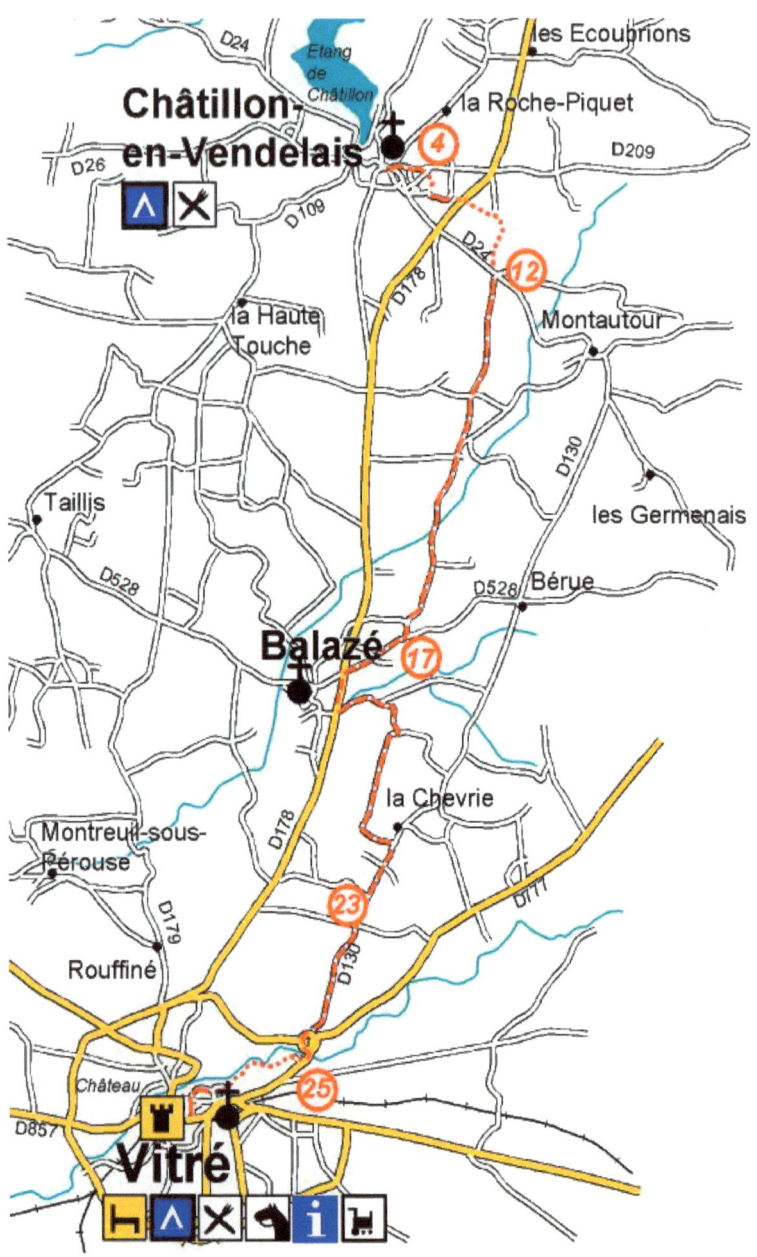

Route Summary: another well marked section offering little difficulty to all groups. There are short sections of main road where it is advisable for walkers and riders to take to the verge. The final entry into Vitré involves a short but steep climb. It is possible to avoid this by remaining on the road at Way Point #25.

Way Point	Distance	Directions	Verification Point	Compass
1		From Place de l'Eglise in Châtillon-en-Vendelais take the D209 in the direction of Princé		E
2	140	Bear left remaining on the D209		E
3	90	Bear right onto rue de Belle Vue	St James sign	E
4	160	Turn right down Passage de la Tuilerie	St James sign	S
5	180	Cross over minor road to continue on the track	St James sign	SE
6	60	Turn left up a grass track with factory on left as you turn	St James sign	NE
7	140	Bear right along the track	St James and GR sign	S
8	200	At T-junction turn left in front of houses to follow the unmade road	St James sign	E
9	150	Continue straight ahead towards farm buildings and then bear right along a narrow track	St James sign	E
10	300	Cross straight over road to continue on grass track on the other side	St James sign	SE
11	400	Keep right with field on left and woods on right	St James sign	S
12	700	Cross straight over the road to continue on the other side direction le Petit Rocher	St James sign	S
13	1600	Continue straight ahead past la Maison Neuve	St James sign	S
14	700	Continue straight ahead, farm on left – le Janvrie	St James sign	S
15	1500	Continue straight ahead	St James sign	SW
16	800	Continue straight ahead	St James sign	S
17	160	At T-junction turn right towards the village of Balazé	St James sign	SW

Châtillon-en-Vendelais to Vitré 16.4km

Way Point	Distance	Directions	Verification Point	Compass
18	900	At crossroads with major road, turn left on D178 direction Vitré. **Note:** walkers and riders keep to the grass verge on the left	St James sign	S
19	500	Turn left onto route de la Bourmenais	St James sign	E
20	600	At fork keep right	St James sign	SE
21	500	Turn right – Mébréhard, les Miaules	St James sign	S
22	2000	At T-junction directly in front of two houses, turn right	St James sign	SW
23	1100	At crossroads continue straight ahead	St James sign	SW
24	1600	At roundabout go straight ahead direction Vitré on D777	St James sign	SW
25	300	Turn right onto a small path opposite houses and just after passing hotel - La Grenoillére. **Note:** there is a wooden barrier across the path, if this causes difficulty for riders then they should continue to follow the D777 to the section end – Way Point #33 at the Office du Tourisme beside the railway station	St James sign	W
26	300	Turn right away from the houses towards the woods	St James sign	W
27	400	Turn right with allotments on right	St James sign	SW
28	200	After steep hill turn right along a narrow passage way in between houses	St James sign	W
29	100	Turn right onto rue du Val de Cantache	St James sign	W
30	50	Continue straight ahead	St James sign	W
31	300	At top of hill turn sharp left and then sharp right to enter town walls and finally enter Place Notre Dame in Vitré	GR sign	E

Châtillon-en-Vendelais to Vitré 16.4km

Way Point	Distance	Directions	Verification Point	Compass
32	70	Leave Place Notre Dame via rue Garengeot	Signs for Office du Tourisme and la Gare	S
33	200	Turn right at traffic island to arrive at the Office du Tourisme	Station on left	

Accommodation - Many options, selection below based on price	Price	Opening	Animals
PR M. et Mme Faucher, 2, chemin des Tertres Noirs 35500 VITRÉ Tel: 0033 (0)2 99 75 08 69 pierre.faucher13@wanadoo.fr bnb.faucher.info	B2	All Year	
L'Espérance, 21, bd des Rochers 35500 VITRÉ Tel: 0033 (0)2 99 75 01 71 restaurant.lesperance@wanadoo.fr	B2	All Year	
Le Petit Billot, 5, Place Général Leclerc 35500 VITRÉ Tel: 0033 (0)2 99 75 02 10 petit-billot@hotel-vitre..com www.petit-billot.com	B2	All Year	
Camping	**Price**	**Opening**	**Animals**
Municipal St-Etienne, Route d'Argentré 35500 VITRÉ Tel: 0033 (0)2 99 75 25 28	B1	All Year	
Camp Municipal Le Clos Ruault 50240 LA CROIX AVRANCHIN Tel: 0033 (0)2 33 48 24 40	B1	All Year	

Equestrian Centre

Etrier Vitréen, 2 allée Cavaliers 35500 VITRE   Tel: 0033 (0)2 99 75 35 03

Useful Contacts

Tourist Offices

Office du Tourisme, pl Gén de Gaulle 35500 VITRE Tel: 0033 (0)2 99 75 04 46
info@ot-vitre.fr   www.ot-vitre.fr/gb/contact.php

Doctor

Juret Jean-Yves, 20 r 70ème RI 35500 VITRE Tel: 0033 (0)2 99 75 06 72

Veterinary

Van Buynderen Pierre, 78 bd Laval 35500 VITRE Tel: 0033 (0)2 99 75 30 90

Farrier

Boutemy André, 2 all Sorbiers 35220 MARPIRE Tel: 0033 (0)2 99 49 76 98

Châtillon-en-Vendelais to Vitré 16.4km

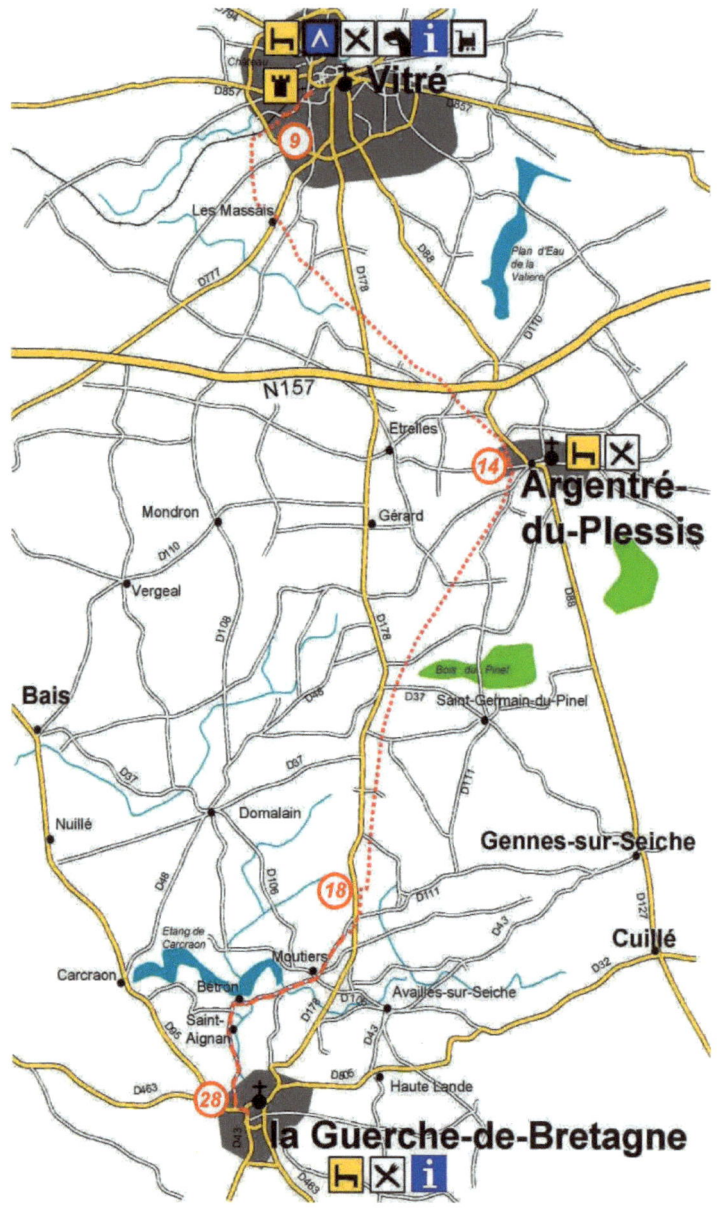

Vitré to La Guerche-de-Bretagne 26.5km

Route Summary: Until Vitré the St James signs have generally indicated direction as well as presence on the route. From there the orientation of the signs is less consistent and can only be interpreted as being on the route. The old railway track ahead makes for very easy going for all groups however there are a number of wooden barriers that may cause some difficulties for horse-riders with large packs.

Way Point	Distance	Directions	Verification Point	Compass
1		From the tourist office return to the traffic island and turn left on rue de Brest	Keep railway line on the left	W
2	70	Bear left on Promenade Saint-Yves, direction Centre Cultural	Keep small park to your right	W
3	300	Turn left onto rue Sainte-Croix	Mont St Michel sign set in the pavement	S
4	300	At the top of the hill bear right onto chemin du Pavillon		SW
5	400	Continue to bear right on the road		W
6	300	Turn left onto a gravel track	Just before the railway tunnel	S
7	100	Fork right into the trees		SW
8	60	Fork right		W
9	130	At the top of the rise turn left along a gravel path. **Note:** Until this point the St James signs have generally indicated direction as well as presence on the route. From here the orientation of the signs is less consistent and can only be interpreted as being on the route. The old railway track ahead makes for very easy going for all groups. However there are a number of wooden barriers that may cause some difficulties for horse-riders with packs.	Railway line close on the right	S
10	3500	Continue straight across the road and around wooden barriers		SE
11	1400	Cross over road to continue on the track	St James sign	SE
12	3100	Follow gravel track to go under road	Wooden barrier	SE
13	130	Rejoin the path on the old railway track	St James sign	SE
14	1300	Cross over main road to continue on the path on the other side	St James sign	S
15	200	Continue straight ahead on small path with large factory buildings on right	Pasquet Menuiserie	SW
16	1300	Cross straight over road beside wooden barriers	St James sign	S
17	7700	After going through wooden barrier continue straight ahead on farm track ignoring left hand fork	St James sign	SW

Vitré to La Guerche-de-Bretagne 26.5km

Vitré to La Guerche-de-Bretagne 26.5km

Way Point	Distance	Directions	Verification Point	Compass
18	200	Turn sharp left through wooden barriers	St James sign, busy road on the right	S
19	600	Cross over major road, D178, and then proceed towards wooden barriers on the other side. After this continue straight ahead on a grass track with a fence on left and minor road to the right	St James sign	SW
20	120	Turn left under a metal arch direction Moutiers	St James sign	SW
21	300	Having gone through playing fields turn left on the road	St James sign	SW
22	900	In Moutiers take right fork into Place Saint Martin and continue on rue du Pont des Arches	St James sign	W
23	700	After crossing bridge turn right onto a smaller road parallel to the main road	St James sign	SW
24	200	At the end of a small picnic area, turn right onto a minor road with house on left as you turn	St James sign	W
25	500	Continue straight ahead avoiding turning to le Colombier	St James sign	SW
26	500	Fork left towards farm buildings and St. Aignan	St James sign	S
27	1800	Cross road straight ahead onto rue de Vignouse and keep right	St James sign	S
28	160	At T-junction, turn left on rue de Rennes towards the centre of la Guerche-de-Bretagne	St James sign	SE
29	200	At roundabout bear right on the D43, direction Angers	St James sign	SE
30	80	Turn left on rue Notre Dame		E
31	130	Arrive in the centre of la Guerche-de-Bretagne at the junction of rue Notre Dame and rue de Nantes beneath statue to St Joseph		

Accommodation	Price	Opening	Animals
Au Cheval Blanc, 1 r Anjou 35370 ARGENTRE DU PLESSIS Tel: 0033 (0)2 99 96 61 30 www.le-chevalblanc.com / hotel.html	B2	All Year	🐴
Hotel La Caleche, 16 avenue du Général Leclerc, 35130 LA GUERCHE-DE-BRETAGNE Tel: 00 33 (0)2 99 96 21 63 contact@lacaleche.com	B2	All Year	🐴
Hôtel des Sports, 2 r Rennes 35130 GUERCHE DE BRETAGNE Tel: 0033 (0)2 99 96 22 11	B2	All Year	🐴
Hôtel-Restaurant Les Routiers, 11 fbg Anjou 35130 GUERCHE DE BRETAGNE Tel: 0033 (0)2 99 96 23 10	B2	All Year	🐴

La Guerche de Bretagne preserves its medieval history with its old houses and its small streets centred around the Basilica Notre-Dame, an ancient collegiate church founded in 1206 by Guillaume II, Lord of the Guerche. Particulary noteworthy are the magnificent spire, renaissance style wooden stalls, 13th century stone recumbent figure of Guillaume II and the 17th century statue of Notre-Dame of The Guerche. Market days (Monday) are particualry colourful and worth setting time aside for.

Useful Contacts

Tourist Offices

La-Guerche-De-Bretagne Office De Tourisme, 30 rue Du Guesclin, 35130 LA GUERCHE-DE-BRETAGNE Tel: 0033 (0)2 99 96 30 78   otsi.laguerche@wanadoo.fr
www.tourisme.fr / office-de-tourisme / la-guerche-de-bretagne.html

Internet Cafes

Archesys, 16 r de L'Union 50100 CHERBOURG Tel: 0033   0(2) 33 53 04 93
eric@endelin.com

Doctor

Hamelin Arnaud, 2 r Sablonnières 35130 LA GUERCHE DE BRETAGNE
Tel: 0033 (0)2 99 96 20 25

Veterinary

Guittot Franck, 6 prom Grand Mail 35130 LA GUERCHE DE BRETAGNE (LA)
Tel: 0033 (0)2 99 96 21 53

Farrier

Le Bihan Gilles, Le Patis 35370 GENNES SUR SEICHE Tel: 0033 (0)2 99 96 80 45

Vitré to La Guerche-de-Bretagne 26.5km

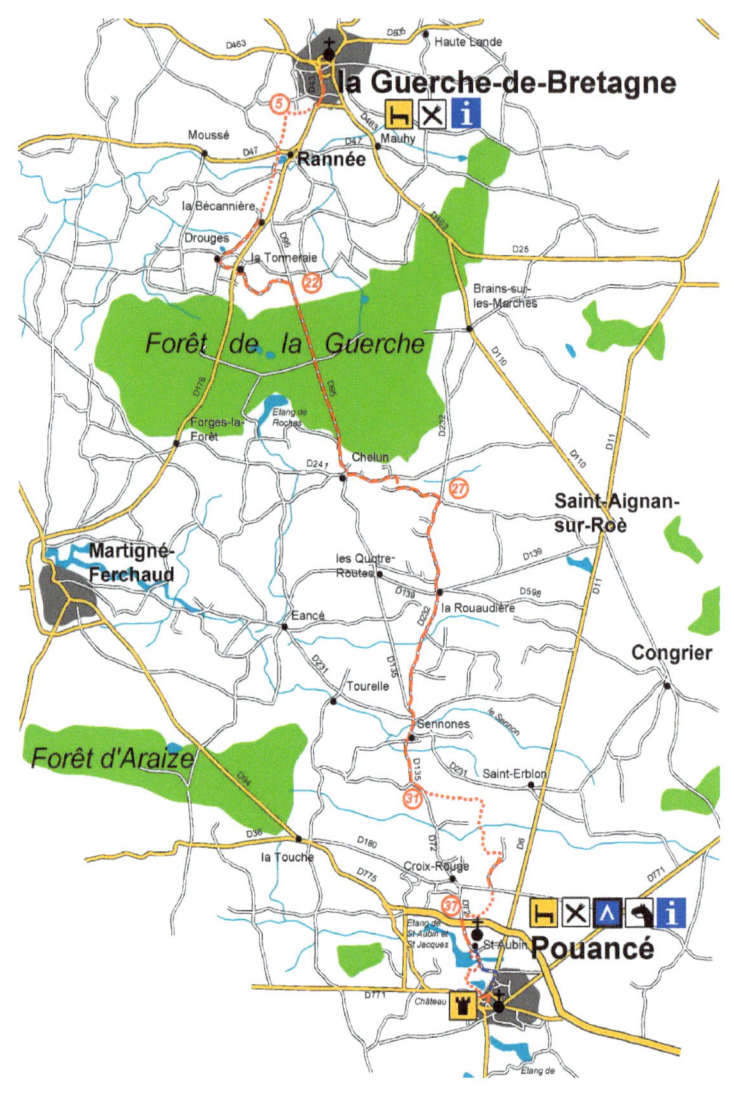

La Guerche-de-Bretagne to Pouancé 32.1km

Route Summary: This segment crosses the Forêt de la Guerche, leaving Brittany and entering the ancient region of Anjou. It is undertaken on mainly level ground with long stretches on generally quiet tarmac roads, interspersed with shorter stretches on farm tracks. The entry into Pouancé for walkers skirts a series of lakes and the town camp-site. While this is a picturesque route it is possible to reduce the distance and eliminate some short steep climbs by following the alternate route suggested for riders. **Note:** A specific pilgrim stamp is obtainable in La Rouadiere, either from the Mairie or the Bar l'Exit. **Look out For:** * statue of St James in L'egilse de la Roudière. * St Aubin de Pouancé - medieval pilgrim cross behind the church and St James lake on right as you cross the bridge.

Way Point	Distance	Directions	Verification Point	Compass
1		From the junction of rue Notre Dame and rue de Nantes take rue de Nantes and continue straight ahead at the crossroads on the D178	Timbered arcade to the right and church to the left	S
2	1000	At roundabout, straight ahead direction Rannée and Châteaubriant, D178	St James sign	SW
3	90	Turn right onto grass track exactly opposite builder's merchants	St James sign	W
4	500	T-junction turn right and continue straight on with farm buildings (la Sallerie) on right	St James sign	W
5	300	Fork left down the hill	St James sign	S
6	900	Turn left onto a minor road	St James sign	SW
7	110	T-junction turn left on the D47	St James sign	SE
8	50	Almost immediately, turn right into a gravelled area and then continue on a grass track with a lake on the left	St James sign	S
9	200	Turn right along a small track that runs beside a barbed wire fence, opposite the weir gate	St James sign	S
10	70	Walkers turn right across a small wooden bridge. **Note:** cyclists and riders continue straight ahead to avoid the bridge and then turn right to rejoin the main track.	St James sign	S
11	200	Cross a minor road and continue straight ahead on the unmade track	St James sign	S
12	800	Keep left on minor road	St James sign	SW
13	300	Continue straight ahead direction Drouges	St James sign	SW
14	130	Keep right with sign for La Grand Bécannière on right	St James sign	SW
15	180	Continue straight ahead towards Drouges avoiding right turn		SW
16	1200	Turn left off rue du Four towards Salle Polyvalente		S
17	110	At crossroads go straight ahead direction Ecole		SE
18	500	Continue straight ahead under the bridge		SE
19	80	At T-junction turn left with house directly in front	La Basse Touche	E
20	90	Turn right direction Chelun	C5	SE
21	700	Remain on road bearing left avoid right turn towards la Feuillée		E

La Guerche-de-Bretagne to Pouancé 32.1km

Way Point	Distance	Directions	Verification Point	Compass
22	900	At T-junction turn right direction Chelun	D95	S
23	4900	Turn left in the middle of Chelun direction Brains sur les Marches. **Note:-** after Chelun the St James signs become much clearer with a yellow background and direction indicator	C3	E
24	70	Continue straight ahead on rue d'Anjou		E
25	1300	Turn right onto farm track direction la Chaire	St James sign	S
26	200	Continue through the farm onto a minor road and then turn left	St James sign	E
27	1300	T-junction turn right	St James sign	S
28	2600	At crossroads in la Rouaudière continue straight ahead direction Senonnes	D232	S
29	3000	AT T-junction turn left direction Senonnes	D135	S
30	800	In Sennones, bear left direction Pouancé	D135	S
31	1500	Turn left onto a grass track between fields towards a radio mast	St James sign	E
32	1600	At T-junction turn right and continue between the trees	St James sign	S
33	90	Bear right at fork in track		S
34	1600	Turn right onto a minor after passing a house on left	La Chênaie	S
35	700	Cross over road to continue on the grass track	St James sign	SW
36	800	Fork right to go between two fields	Main road on left	W
37	300	Turn left on rue Saint-Jacques	Pass under road bridge	S
38	700	Bear left into Saint-Aubin		SE
39	200	Turn right into a gravelled area just before reaching the church. **Note:-** the route ahead involves a number of flights of steps before reaching the centre of Pouancé. Horse and bike riders should remain on the road and continue in the direction of Pouancé. At the T-junction turn right on rue de la Gare, entering the centre of the town at Way Point #49 on rue Saint Aubin	St James sign	SW
40	40	Cross a small yard and continue straight ahead towards the lake and then bear slightly left after going through a barrier with a chain across	St James sign	SW

La Guerche-de-Bretagne to Pouancé 32.1km

Way Point	Distance	Directions	Verification Point	Compass
41	70	Turn left beside Etang de Saint Aubin et Saint Jacques	Keep lake to the right	SE
42	170	At junction with rue de l'Hippodrome turn right and cross the bridge		S
43	140	After crossing bridge bear right on a track keeping lake on right	Beside camping area	SW
44	300	After passing a barrier turn left	Children's playground on the left	S
45	120	Continue straight ahead up the flight of wooden steps		S
46	40	Cross disused railway track and descend embankment. Follow path with lake to your left		SE
47	600	Bear left on small road	Lake to the left	SE
48	110	Mount steps towards the old château and turn left on the boulevard du Vieux Château	Keep château to your right	NE
49	200	At the crossroads turn right rue Saint Aubin		S
50	200	Turn left on rue Porte de Angevine		E
51	60	Arrive in the centre of Pouancé beside the Tourist Office		

Accommodation	Price	Opening	Animals
Hotel Restaurant La Porte Angevine, 1 r Roger Pironneau 49420 POUANCÉ Tel: 0033 (0)2 41 92 68 52	B2	All Year	🐴
La Porte Angevine, 1 r Roger Pironneau 49420 POUANCÉ Tel: 0033 (0)2 41 92 68 52	B2	All Year	🐴

Camping	Price	Opening	Animals
Camping Municipal, 23 r Etangs 49420 POUANCÉ Mobile: 0033 (0)6 18 69 96 43 info@ville-pouance.fr	B1	March-Oct	🐴
Camping Municipal Roche Martin, 23 r Etangs 49420 POUANCE Tel: 0033 (0)2 41 61 98 79	B1	All Year	🐴

Equestrian Centre

Maison Familiale Hippique, 6 r Tresse 49420 POUANCÉ Tel: 0033 (0)2 41 92 43 28

Ferme Equestre, Le Refuge Coconneries 49420 POUANCE   Tel: 0033 (0)2 41 61 78 12

Denis Alain, Fresne 49420 POUANCE   Tel: 0033 (0)2 41 92 67 26

La Guerche-de-Bretagne to Pouancé 32.1km

Pouancé is a small, but interesting town, which deserves setting time aside for. It is dominated by its two churches – the church of the Madeleine (probably most notable for its organ, built by Louis Bonn and installed in 1864) and the church of Saint-Aubin (particularly interesting for its vault, which is covered with splendid and recently renovated mural frescos). More controversially, it is also home to one of the few remaining Grenier à Sel, a painful reminder of the gabelle.

The term gabelle derives from the Latin term gabulum (a tax) and it became one of the most hated and most grossly unequal taxes in the country, but, though condemned by all supporters of reform, it was not abolished until 1790. Greniers à Sel (salt granaries dating from 1342)

were established in each province, and to these all salt had to be taken by the producer on penalty of confiscation. The grenier fixed the price which it paid for the salt and then sold it to retail dealers at a higher rate.

There were six distinct groups of provinces and the differences in cost between these fostered the practice of buying salt in a region where it was cheap and selling it illegally in regions where it was expensive. Such smugglers were called faux-sauniers (from faux – false and the root sau-, referring to salt). In turn, the customs guards tasked with arresting the faux-sauniers were nicknamed gabelous. Faux-sauniers were sentenced to the galleys if they were caught without weapons, and to death if caught with weapons. In 1675, the red bonnets in Brittany rebelled against the gabelle and it was eventually repealed.

The name **Segré** is believed to come from the latin "Secretum" which means "isolated", but in fact tribes, attracted by the fertile land, have settled here since pre-Roman times. More recently, Segré was the capital of the local slate and iron mining region, but today tourism and lighter, local industries predominate.

La Madeleine, a neo-Byzantine church, built in 1838, has undergone numerous modifications. The 22 metre long choir supporting a 30 metre high dome was designed by the architect Delletre, who also built a second church tower. The stained glass windows, which are listed, are the work of Clamens, and they date back to the XIXth Century ; the three stained glass windows of the choir relate to the three main moments in St Magdalen's life ; the other three represent the Patron Saints of some private donors and of St Francis' Third Order. The organ, bearing the signature of Cavaillé-Coll, dates back to 1881.

Pouancé to Segré 38.8km

Pouancé to Segré 38.8km

Route Summary: This is a long section on a mix of green lanes and generally minor roads. There is the opportunity to find accommodation at a number of villages along the section and also to reduce the overall distance by almost 6 kilometres by taking the alternate routes to avoid the less direct sections of pathway.

Way Point	Distance	Directions	Verification Point	Compass
1		From the door of the tourist office turn left along rue de la Porte Angevine	Travelling away from the archway	SE
2	30	At the crossroads with the main road - rue de la Libération – go straight ahead. **Note:-** the signed route differs slightly over the next 200 metres, but to no advantage. To reduce route distance by 2 kilometres take the alternate route to the left and exit Pouancé on the D181, Avenue Général Leclerc, direction Vergonnes and Segré. After passing the sports grounds and the château/hospital turn right direction Armaillé and take the track on the left after 150 metres – Way Point #19		S
3	150	At the T-junction turn right on boulevard du Champ de Foire	Pass high walls and steps on the right	SW
4	300	At the mini-roundabout bear left on the D878	Direction Prévière	S
5	300	Turn left on the small road directly opposite rue de la Laiterie	Signed sentier de Tressé	E
6	100	Cross the wooden bridge and turn right	St James sign on the bridge	SE
7	400	Bear left and follow the path beside the lake	Keep lake to the right	E
8	500	At T-junction of tracks turn right towards the lake and then left	Keep lake to the right	E
9	300	At T-junction with tarmac road turn right		SE
10	200	At crossroads continue straight ahead		SE
11	150	Continue straight ahead through wooden gate	Sign Sentier des Ecureuils	NE
12	600	Bear right on the track to bypass the château	Pass green garage on the left	N
13	100	Bear left in the better defined track towards the château	St James sign	W
14	50	At T-junction turn right away from the château		N
15	90	Continue straight ahead	Chapel to the right	NW
16	120	Exit through château gates and bear right	St James sign	N

Pouancé to Segré 38.8km

Way Point	Distance	Directions	Verification Point	Compass
17	60	At zebra crossing turn right on track	St James sign	NE
18	300	Bear right away from the château and towards the road	Sports ground on the left	N
19	20	Cross the road and take the pathway opposite	St James sign	E
20	1400	At crossroads continue straight ahead	La Coconnerie	E
21	1100	Keep left and remain parallel to the main road D775	Hamlet of la Gaudie to the right	E
22	1400	Continue straight ahead beside the main road. **Note:-** major roadworks were taking place at the time of writing. In the event of disruption to the route follow sign-posts to Grugé-l'Hôpital and synchronize with the route at Way Point #32	Main road now close on the left	E
23	160	Turn left to cross the main road and proceed on the left side		E
24	300	Turn left on route des Grées	Direction Chazé Henry	NE
25	300	Turn right on track	St James sign	E
26	400	At junction with road go straight ahead		E
27	80	At bend in the road continue straight ahead on the track	St James sign	E
28	1100	At road junction turn right towards Vergonnes		S
29	500	At the junction with the main road in Vergonnes turn left and pass through the village	Proceed on main road towards Segré	E
30	700	After leaving Vergonnes turn left on the D212 towards la Chapelle-Hullin	St James sign	N
31	500	Beside la Haute Lande turn right towards Grugé-l'Hôpital	Towards Fôret Dombrée	NE
32	4300	At the road junction beside the church in Grugé-l'Hôpital turn right on the D180	Towards Bouillé-Ménard	E
33	300	At the fork in the road bear right. **Note:** to reduce route length by 3.7 kilometres bear left to take the alternate route and follow the D180 to Bouillé-Ménard and the D71 to Nyoiseau rejoining the main route at Way Point #59	Beside cemetry	SE

Pouancé to Segré 38.8km

Way Point	Distance	Directions	Verification Point	Compass
34	2000	At the T-junction turn left	Village of Bourg l'Evêque to the right	N
35	170	Turn right towards la Ruaudière	St James sign	NE
36	1400	At junction with the D180 turn right	Towards Bouillé-Ménard	SE
37	1200	Beside signs for la Barre and la Petite Barre, take the third track (grass) to the right	Towards the left side of the farm buildings, St James sign	SW
38	200	Having passed around the farm buildings bear left up the hill on the grassy track	Small yellow arrow	S
39	300	At the bottom of the hill join a small tarmac road and continue straight ahead	La Saulnerie to the right	SE
40	900	At T-junction turn left	St James sign	E
41	140	Immediately before an electricity transformer turn right on a grass track	St James sign	SW
42	700	Track emerges onto tarmac driveway bear left	Metal gates on the right	S
43	40	At T-junction turn left	St James sign	E
44	300	Shortly before reaching la Buquinnière turn right on a gravelled track	Turning 30 metres before 2 blue gate posts on the right	S
45	90	At fork in the track bear right and then immediately left	St James sign	S
46	300	At junction with road turn left on the tarmac road towards the village of la Chapelle aux Pies	St James sign	SE
47	300	At crossroads in la Chapelle aux Pies continue straight ahead on rue des Fauvettes	St James sign	E
48	1500	At the crossroads turn right on the D219 direction Noyant la Gravoyère	St James sign	S
49	1100	Just before leaving the village of Misengrains turn left towards la Mine Bleue	St James sign	E
50	1600	Immediately in front of the Bio Pig Farm, la Prévoté turn right on track	St James sign	S

Pouancé to Segré 38.8km

Way Point	Distance	Directions	Verification Point	Compass
51	80	Turn left into field keeping hedge close on your left side. **Note:** the track ahead is blocked to horse-riders by a fallen tree. Horse-riders should continue straight ahead, then bear left beside the first lake Etang de St-Blaise. At the foot of the hill cross to the right side of the second lake Etang de la Corbinière, following the track beside the lake until reaching the road where they should turn left towards la Croix Malard and rejoin the main track at Way Point #54	Mont St Michel sign on post to the right	E
52	50	With water tower and pithead visible on the right bear left into a green lane		E
53	600	Crossroads in tracks continue straight ahead		E
54	800	At junction with road bear left	St James sign	E
55	170	Take the right fork on the slightly smaller road towards le Marchais Lavoir	Mont St Michel sign on the left	E
56	600	As road bends to the right turn left on green lane	Small partly obscured metal crucifix on the left	NE
57	200	At junction with tarmac road turn right	St James sign	E
58	400	In Nyoiseau at crossroads continue straight ahead on rue de l'Eglise	St James sign, and church to the left	E
59	90	At crossroads with the Mairie ahead turn right on the main road	Direction Segré	S
60	600	Turn left on the small road towards the château and college d'Orveau parallel to to the river Oudon	St James sign	E
61	300	Continue straight ahead passing camp-site on the left		SE
62	300	At crossroads continue straight ahead passing the château to the left	Remain parallel to the river	E
63	1200	Turn right towards the village of Souvray	St James sign	S
64	140	Bear left with quarry on the left		S
65	500	At the crossroads turn left towards St Aubin du Pavoil	St James sign	E
66	1500	At T-junction turn right towards the village centre		S
67	200	Bear left to pass in front of the church		SE

Pouancé to Segré 38.8km

Way Point	Distance	Directions	Verification Point	Compass
68	30	Bear right on Allée du Moulin. **Note:-** to avoid the metal bridge ahead take the alternate route to the left on rue du Lavoir, after crossing the river, turn right beside the crucifix in la Planchette and rejoin the main route at Way Point #71 beside Bellevue		S
69	200	Cross the Oudon on an iron bridge		SE
70	90	Bear left and climb the hill	Mill on the left	E
71	150	At T-junction turn right towards Segré	St James sign	S
72	200	Continue straight ahead on rue de Court Pivert	Pass under main road	S
73	800	At crossroads continue straight ahead on rue du Pinelier		S
74	700	At crossroads turn left on rue du Calvaire		E
75	100	At crossroads turn right on rue Voltaire		S
76	70	Bear right on rue de la Madeleine		SW
77	60	Turn left on rue Joulain		S
78	70	On reaching the river turn right and then left to cross the river bridge and enter rue Victor Hugo		S
79	50	Arrive in the centre of Segré at the junction of rue Victor Hugo and rue Hoche		

Pouancé to Segré 38.8km

Accommodation	Price	Opening	Animals
La Ruadiére 49520 GRUGE l'HOPITAL Tel: 0033 (0)2 41 61 63 15 **Note:** only accommodates groups	B1	All Year	
Relais De Misengrain, 20 Misengrain 49520 NOYANT LA GRAVOYERE Tel: 0033 (0)2 41 61 51 10 cat.du.haut-anjou@wanadoo.fr www.cat-haut-anjou.com **Note:** only accommodates groups	B2	All Year	
Fleur-d-Ecosse, 2 rue de L'eglise 49520 NOYANT LA GRAVOYERE Tel: 0033 (0)2 41 61 41 86	B2	All Year	
La Prévoté 49520 NOYANT LA GRAVOYERE Tel: 0033 (0)9 61 51 57 67 c.sheard@wanadoo.fr	B2	All Year	
Hauts des Brèges 49500 NYOISEAU Tel: 0033 (0)2 41 61 39 07 b.pellier@wanadoo.fr www.hauts-de-breges.com	B2	All Year	
PR Hôtel Le Segré, r Gustave Eiffel 49500 SEGRE Tel: 0033 (0)2 41 94 81 81	B2	All Year	
Le Plessis, 4 pl Eglise St Aubin Pavoil 49500 SEGRÉ Tel: 0033 (0)2 41 92 85 03 domainevitton@wanadoo.fr	B2	All Year	

Camping	Price	Opening	Animals
Camping Le Segre, Rue de la Couloumine 66800 SAILLAGOUSE Tel: 0033 (0)4 68 04 74 72		01/01- 31/12	

Equestrian Centre
Centre Equestre Municipal; r 8 Mai 1945 49500 SEGRE Tel: 0033 (0)2 41 92 23 09

Useful Contacts

Tourist Offices

Office de Tourisme du Canton de Segré, 5 rue David d'Angers 49500 SEGRE
Tel: 0033 (0)2 41 92 86 83

Internet Cafes

Le Dartagnan, Renaissance 49500 SEGRE Tel: 0033 (0)2 41 92 27 86
L'Escale, 18 r Gambetta 49500 SEGRE Tel: 0033 (0)2 41 61 09 48
Café de la Mairie, 19 pl Aristide Briand 49500 SEGRE Tel: 0033 (0)2 41 92 30 10

Doctor

De La Garoullaye Henry, 1 Vieille Rue 49520 NOYANT LA GRAVOYERE
Tel: 0033 (0)2 41 61 50 81

Veterinary

Ameloot Hérvé, zi rte Aviré 49500 SEGRE Tel: 0033 (0)2 41 94 74 74

Farrier

Sourice Patrick, 42 r Val d'Hommée 49220 VERN D'ANJOU
Tel: 0033 (0)2 41 61 43 05

Pouancé to Segré 38.8km

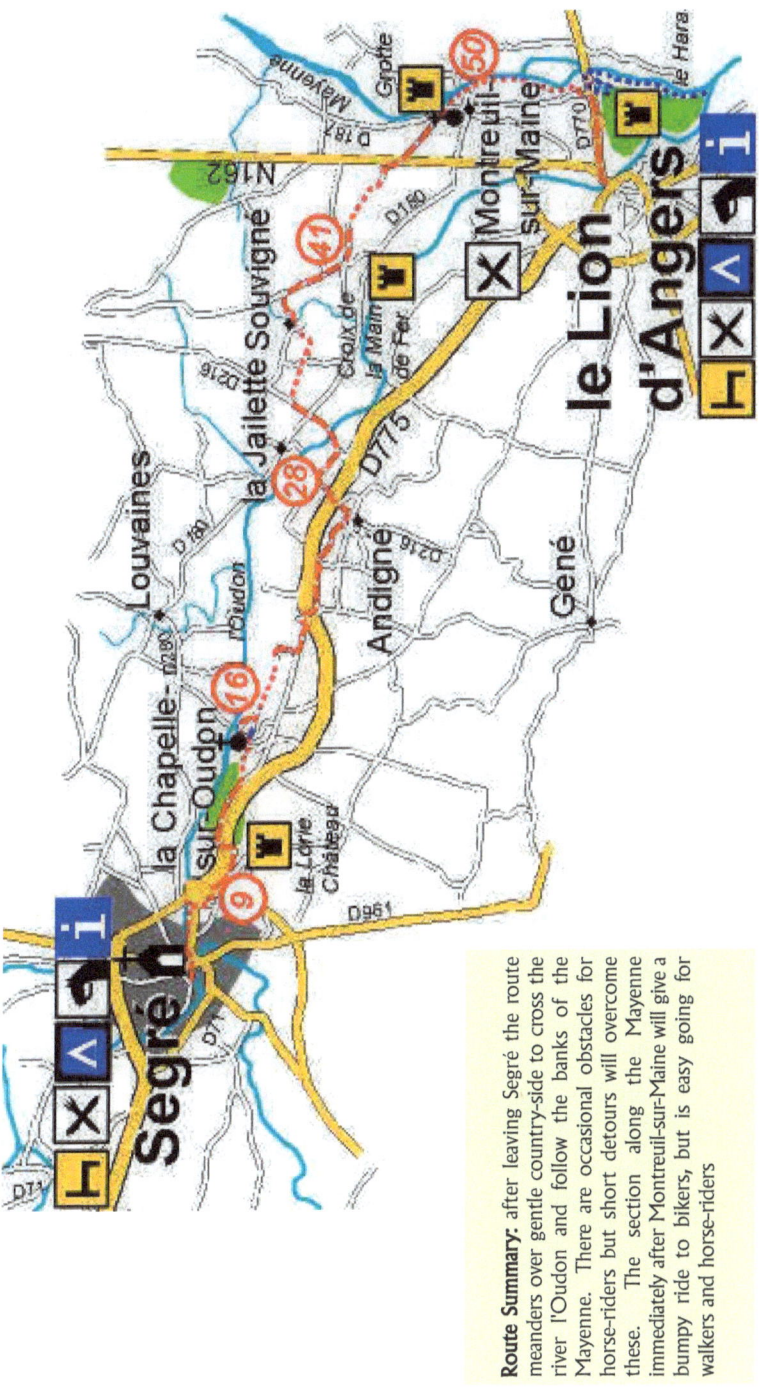

Route Summary: after leaving Segré the route meanders over gentle country-side to cross the river l'Oudon and follow the banks of the Mayenne. There are occasional obstacles for horse-riders but short detours will overcome these. The section along the Mayenne immediately after Montreuil-sur-Maine will give a bumpy ride to bikers, but is easy going for walkers and horse-riders

Segré to le-Lion-d'Angers 21.5km

Way Point	Distance	Directions	Verification Point	Compass
1		From the junction at the end of the bridge continue along rue Victor Hugo		E
2	300	Straight on at the crossroads, rue David d'Angers, and then turn left in front of the Credit Agricole bank towards the river-side	St James sign, Tourist Office on right	NE
3	110	Continue straight ahead keeping the river on left	St James sign	E
4	200	Straight ahead onto a grass track	St James sign, and river on left	E
5	600	Turn right up a flight of steps directly under the road bridge. **Note:-** For horse-riders and cyclists there is a parallel track leading to the top of the steps just 10 metres ahead	St James sign	S
6	30	At the top of the steps continue straight ahead up a small grass track	St James sign and bridge on the left	SE
7	60	At the top of the hill bear right towards a telephone box	St James sign	S
8	70	Cross over main road and turn left towards a large traffic island	St James sign and archways to right	SE
9	180	At roundabout take second exit direction Château de la Lorie	St James sign	SE
10	300	At fork in road keep left and pass under the main road and continue with the main road now to your right	St James sign	E
11	800	Fork left taking the second left grass track	St James sign and wooden crucifix on left	E
12	1300	In la-Chapelle-sur-Oudon turn left with the church straight ahead. **Note:-** the path ahead includes a flight of slippery steps. Horse-riders are advised to continue straight ahead remaining parallel to the river to rejoin the main route after 350 metres at Way Point #16	St James sign	NE
13	50	Turn right down ruelle du Rocher	St James sign	E
14	110	At bottom of steps turn left and immediately right beside the river	St James sign	E
15	200	At the end of the gravelled track fork right	St James sign	S
16	300	At the top of the hill turn left on chemin de Paradis	St James sign	E
17	140	Track forks, keep right	St James sign	SE

Segré to le-Lion-d'Angers 21.5km

Way Point	Distance	Directions	Verification Point	Compass
18	500	Path comes up to hedge, turn right with hedge on left and then shortly after turn left again between hedges	St James sign	E
19	500	Track comes out onto a minor road, continue straight ahead	St James sign and farm track to left	E
20	200	Take right fork towards les Guadines du Milieu	St James sign	S
21	300	At junction with a major road, turn left with les Guadines Basses directly ahead	St James sign	E
22	500	At the roundabout take second exit and cross the bridge direction Le Lion d'Anger	St James sign	S
23	130	At the second roundabout take the second exit direction Andigné	St James sign	E
24	1700	Turn right just before entering Andigné	St James sign	SE
25	190	Turn left onto rue de la Main de Fer	St James sign	NE
26	160	Continue straight ahead onto rue St Aubin with the church to your right	St James sign	NE
27	150	At crossroads go straight ahead onto rue de l'Oudon	St James sign	NE
28	500	300 metres after crossing the highway take the right fork	St James sign	SE
29	500	At crossroads turn first left onto a minor road towards Port-aux-Anglais. **Note:-** horse-riders go straight ahead to rejoin the main route at Way Point #32 just before the river bridge	St James sign	NE
30	200	Turn right with river on left	St James sign	SE
31	50	Take flight of steps up to the road	St James sign	E
32	20	At the top of the steps turn left to cross over a bridge	St James sign	NE
33	500	At crossroads continue straight ahead direction St-Martin-du-Bois on the D216	St James sign	NE
34	400	Turn right onto unmade track, with orchards on right	St James sign	E
35	600	Turn right and then immediately left direction la Grand Chênaie	St James sign	SE
36	110	Continue straight ahead with farm building, la Grand Chênaie, on right	St James sign	NE
37	600	Track comes out onto a minor road, turn right with house, Souvigné, directly on right	St James sign	E

Segré to le-Lion-d'Angers 21.5km

Way Point	Distance	Directions	Verification Point	Compass
38	50	Continue straight ahead onto a grass track with the house directly to your right	St James sign	E
39	500	At junction with a minor road, turn right	St James sign	S
40	700	Continue straight ahead	St James sign	SE
41	300	At crossroads, turn left direction les Noyers	St James sign	E
42	300	Go straight ahead through a farm yard and onto a grass track	St James sign	E
43	400	At fork in the track, keep right	St James sign	SE
44	1200	At junction with a major road, turn right	St James sign	S
45	140	Turn left down a minor road direction Montreuil-sur-Maine	St James sign	SE
46	900	Turn right towards Montreuil-sur-Maine on D187	St James sign	SE
47	80	Turn left towards a crucifix, the river and la Grotte. **Note:-** horse-riders remain on the D187 until reaching the crossroads in Montreuil-sur-Maine, then turn left to rejoin the main route at Way Point #50 on the river-side	St James sign	NE
48	40	At the bottom of the flight of steps turn right with river on left	St James sign	SE
49	300	Continue straight ahead		SE
50	200	Take left fork to remain close to the river, church on right	St James sign	S
51	1500	After a long stretch through fields continue straight into a wood towards houses ahead	St James sign	S
52	90	Bear right up the hill	St James sign	S
53	300	Grass track comes onto a minor road, turn right up the hill with a large factory on the right	St James sign	W
54	180	T-junction turn left to go down the hill	St James sign	SE

Segré to le-Lion-d'Angers 21.5km

Way Point	Distance	Directions	Verification Point	Compass
55	160	T-junction turn right direction Segré on D770. **Note:-** if you do not wish to visit the town of le Lion-d'Angers the journey can be reduced by 2.5 kilometres by taking the alternate route along the towpath (chemin de haulage) on the right bank of the river Mayenne. For this route go straight ahead through the entrance to Le Haras National du Domaine de l'Isle Briand passing the automatic barrier. After approximately 80 metres turn left, with hedge on your left and follow the yellow signs for chemin de haulage, proceed down the hill following the signs to the riverside, then turn right and proceed to the footbridge over the river l'Oudon at Way Point #6 of the next section. In the event that le Haras is closed, pedestrians can turn left towards the road bridge and descend to the riverside by a steep flight of steps behind the crash barriers on the right.		W
56	900	At roundabout take third exit in the direction of Segré		W
57	400	At a major junction turn left direction Centre Ville		SW
58	300	After crossing a bridge, arrive in le Lion-d'Angers at the crossroads beside the Hotel les Voyageurs		

Segré to le-Lion-d'Angers 21.5km

Accommodation	Price	Opening	Animals
Maison Familiale Rural, 2 rue des Sources 49220 LE LION D'ANGERS Tel: 0033 (0)2 41 96 91 60	B1	All Year	❌
Travaillères 49220 LE LION D'ANGERS Tel: 0033 (0)2 41 61 33 56 www.lestravailleres.com	B2	All Year	✓
PR Hôtel des Voyageurs, 2 r Gén Leclerc 49220 Le LION D'ANGERS Tel: 0033 (0)2 41 05 08 66	B2	All Year	✓

Camping	Price	Opening	Animals
Camping Municipal, rte Château-Gontier 49220 le LION D'ANGERS Tel: 0033 (0)2 41 95 31 56	B1	All Year	✓

Equestrian Centre

Hippodrome L'Isle Briand, lieu-dit L'Isle Briand 49220 LION D'ANGERS
Tel: 0033 (0)2 41 95 32 79

Useful Contacts

Tourist Offices

Office De Tourisme Le Lion d'Angers, Square des Villes Jumelées 49220 LE LION-D'ANGERS   Tel: 0033 (0)2 41 95 83 19   otintercom-leliondangers@wanadoo.fr

Doctor

Javelot Thierry, 1 quai Bretagne   49220 Le LION D'ANGERS
Tel: 0033 (0)2 41 95 31 45

Veterinary

Tesson Cyrille, 9 av Acacias 49220 Le LION D'ANGERS   Tel: 0033 (0)2 41 95 30 96

Farrier

Neveu Franck, 1 rte Grez Neuville 49220 THORIGNE D'ANJOU
Tel: 0033 (0)2 41 95 45 56

Route Summary: with the exception of the short but strenuous climb from the river-side into the centre of Montreuil-Juigné this is a flat easy segment with much of the journey spent on pathways beside the river. The entry and the later completion of the crossing of the city of Angers is undertaken on generally safe river-side tracks passable by all groups.

Way Point	Distance	Directions	Verification Point	Compass
1		From the road junction beside the Hôtel Les Voyageurs in le Lion-d'Angers, recross the bridge towards the Haras and the race course	D770 towards Segré	NE

Way Point	Distance	Directions	Verification Point	Compass
2	60	At the end of the bridge turn right onto the riverside path. **Note:-** on race days the path will be closed from early morning until late evening. As an alternative retrace your approach to le Lion-d'Angers remaining on the D770 until Way Point #55 of the previous section at the entrance to the Haras. Continue from there on the alternate route	Between race course and the river	SE
3	900	After crossing the wooden bridge and climbing the short steep hill bear right on the broader track	Turning away from the race course	SE
4	190	Bear right on the small lower track closer to the river		S
5	400	At fork in the track bear right remaining closer to the river		SE
6	800	At T-junction, beside the point where l'Oudon and Mayenne merge, turn right over the metal bridge. **Note:-** the alternate route rejoins from the left	Bridge crosses l'Oudon	S
7	2000	In the village of Grez-Neuville continue straight ahead on the river-side and pass under the road bridge	Créperie to the right	SE
8	3500	At the boat launching ramp beside the boat-yard continue straight ahead with the camp-site on the right and the river on the left	St James sign	SE
9	200	At the ferry jetty turn right and immediately left into the car park. Exit the far side of the car park through a wood and metal gate continuing along the river-side	Metal wind powered water pump ahead on the right	SE
10	1100	In the car park before the Ecluse de la Roussière turn right onto the tarmac road running at right angles to the river	St James sign	S
11	300	Turn left on the road in the direction of Montreuil-Juigné		SE

Le-Lion-d'Angers to Angers 28.6km

Way Point	Distance	Directions	Verification Point	Compass
12	4500	Just before the T-junction with the D103 turn left onto a gravel path. **Note:-** the path ahead proceeds by the side of the river Mayenne. There are steep sections and a fallen tree partially blocking the path (at the time of writing) to avoid these obstructions it is possible to turn left on the D103 at the T-junction and follow rue Saint-Jean-Baptiste, avenue du Président Kennedy and rue Anatole France before turning left into place de la République and rejoining the main route beside the church at Way Point #27	Cemetery on the left	SE
13	160	After crossing the car park turn left onto the track and towards the wooden barriers	Turn beside the school	E
14	70	Turn right onto the gravel path beside the river	River on the left	S
15	180	After passing through the wooden barriers bear left	St James sign	SE
16	140	Bear right keeping the river close on the left	St James sign	SW
17	200	After passing under the road bridge continue on the narrow path	River on the left	S
18	400	Continue straight ahead into woodland	Keep river close on the left	SE
19	500	Turn right up a short flight of steps	St James sign	SE
20	30	At the top of the steps continue straight ahead keeping the fence and river on the left		SE
21	170	Bear left down the hill. **Note:-** there was a fallen tree across the pass at the time of writing	St James sign	SE
22	40	Continue straight ahead up the hill	St James sign	S
23	20	Turn left up the hill		E
24	50	Turn right and then immediately left		SW
25	20	At the top of the hill turn right towards a large white building		S
26	20	Bear right on the tarmac road to pass close beside the large modern church of Saint Etienne on your left	Parc François Mitterand sign	S
27	130	At the junction with the main road turn left with the church on the left	Towards pharmacy	E

Le-Lion-d'Angers to Angers 28.6km

Le-Lion-d'Angers to Angers 28.6km

Way Point	Distance	Directions	Verification Point	Compass
28	110	Turn right on rue de David d'Angers	St James sign	S
29	170	At the mini-roundabout continue straight ahead on rue de David d'Angers	St James sign	S
30	300	At the mini-roundabout take the last exit onto avenue des Poiriers	St James sign	SE
31	400	At the mini-roundabout continue straight ahead direction cimetière		SE
32	160	Bear right onto a gravel track with the entrance to the cemetery on the left	St James sign	SE
33	140	Take the right fork onto a narrow track between 2 large stones		SE
34	700	At the road junction turn right	St James sign	SE
35	190	At the top of a small rise bear left onto a gravel track	St James sign	SE
36	80	Take the left fork on a gravel track	St James sign	E
37	300	At a T-junction in the track turn left in the direction of Cantenay-Epinard	St James sign	N
38	400	At junction with a minor road turn right	St James sign	NE
39	120	Turn left onto a track direction of Cantenay-Epinard	St James sign and wooden barrier	N
40	600	At the wooden barrier turn right with a wire fence on the left		NE
41	600	Cross straight over the road to continue on the track	St James sign	NE
42	200	Beside iron gate turn right through a wooden barrier	St James sign	SE
43	800	At the fork in the track continue straight ahead keeping the river on the left		SE
44	300	At the junction with the busy D107 turn left towards the river bridge	St James sign	E
45	50	Immediately before the bridge turn right on a narrow river-side track	River on the left	S

Way Point	Distance	Directions	Verification Point	Compass
46	2100	Cross the parking area and bear left to join the narrow river-side track	Red and yellow sign	SE
47	300	Cross the minor road and continue on the river-side track	Red and yellow sign	SE
48	300	Cross the minor road leading to the ferry and continue on the river-side track	Wooden barrier	SE
49	1800	Continue straight ahead beside the river to pass under 3 bridges	The Mayenne and Sarthe rivers merge on the left to form the Maine	SW
50	600	Take the lower track beside the river	Red and yellow sign	SW
51	900	Bear right briefly to leave the river and proceed on rue Larrey in front of the Centre Hospitalier Universitaire d'Angers		SW
52	200	Bear left to rejoin the path beside the river	Shortly after passing the rowing club Club Angers Nautique	SE
53	70	Turn left to take the lower path keeping the river to the left		SW
54	600	The path climbs a ramp away from the river, continue straight ahead on the road Quai Robert Fèvre		SW
55	70	Arrive in Angers centre at the junction between Quai Robert Fèvre and Pont de Verdun	Across the river from Cathédrale Saint-Maurice d'Angers	

Useful Contacts

Tourist Offices
ANGERS LOIRE TOURISME, G Pl Kennedy 49051 ANGERS
Tel: 0033 (0)2 41 23 50 00   www.angersloiretourisme.com / EN / index2.aspx
accueil@angersloiretourisme.com

Internet Cafes
Ambiances Multimédia, 10 r Bodinier 49100 ANGERS   Tel: 0033 (0)2 41 18 26 24
contact@ambiances-multimedia.com

Doctor
Beaussier Philippe, 238 av Pasteur 49000 ANGERS Tel: 0033 (0)2 41 43 70 47

Veterinary
Clinique Vétérinaire, 81 r Meignanne 49100 ANGERS   Tel: 0033 (0)2 41 88 12 13

Farrier
Geray Pascal, Les Justeries chem Landes 49800 TRELAZE   Tel: 0033 (0)2 41 34 12 15

Le-Lion-d'Angers to Angers 28.6km

Accommodation (large choice of hotels in Angers)	Price	Opening	Animals
Manoir du bois de Grez, Le Bois de Grez Route de Sceaux d'Anjou 49220 GREZ NEUVILLE Tel: 0033 (0)2 41 18 00 09 Mobile: 0033 (0)6 22 38 14 56	B2	All Year	🐴
LA CROIX D'ETAIN, 2 Rue de l'Ecluse 49220 GREZ-NEUVILLE Tel : OO33 (0)2 41 95 68 49	B3	All Year	🐴
Le Plateau, rue Espéranto 49460 MONTREUIL-JUIGNE Tel: 0033 (0)2 41 42 32 35	B2	All Year	🐴
Hôtel Continental, 14 Rue Louis De Romain 49100 ANGERS Tel: 0033 (0)2 41 86 94 94 reservation@hotellecontinental.com	B2	All Year	🐴
Ethic Etapes Lac de Maine, 49 Avenue du lac de Maine 49100 ANGERS Tel: 0033 (0)2 41 22 32 10	B1	All Year	🐴
Hôtel Le Progrès, 26 av Denis Papin 49100 ANGERS Tel: 0033 (0)2 41 88 10 14	B3	All Year	🐴

Accommodation in Religious Houses	Price	Opening	Animals
Le Bon Pasteur, 3 rue Brault (near the church of St Jacques) 49100 ANGERS Tel: 0033 (0)2 41 72 12 80	B1	All Year	❌

Youth Hostel	Price	Opening	Animals
Foyer Darwin, 3 rue Darwin 49100 ANGERS Tel: 0033 (0)2 41 22 61 20 www.foyerdarwin.com / sommaire.html	B1	All Year	❌

Camping	Price	Opening	Animals
Camping Municipal, Place du Bac 49220 PRUILLE Tel: 0033 (0)2 41 32 67 29	B1	All Year	🐴
Camping Municipal Leon-Delanoue, rue de Président Kennedy, 49460 MONTREUIL-JUIGNE Tel: 0033 (0)2 41 41 40 18	B1	All Year	🐴
Camping du lac de Maine, Avenue du Lac de Maine 49100 ANGERS Tel: 0033 (0)2 41 73 05 03	B1	25/03 - 10/10	🐴

Equestrian Centre
Poney club de La Tinière 49220 GREZ-NEUVILLE   Tel: 0033 (0)2 41 95 26 82
Le Domaine d'Olisun, Montigné 49220 PRUILLÉ Tel: 0033 (0)2 41 32 64 89 Mobile: 0033 (0)6 62 42 64 89
Feron Marjorie, 10 sq Eugène Pottier 49000 ANGERS   Mobile: 0033 (0)6 16 26 76 63

Angers is located in the French region known by its pre-revolutionary, provincial name, Anjou, and its inhabitants are called Angevins. The city traces its roots to early Roman times. It occupies both banks of the Maine, which is spanned by six bridges. The district along the river is famous for its flourishing nurseries and market gardens. It is well known for its fresh produce and cut flowers.

Angers was once the capital of the historic province of Anjou. Beginning in the ninth century, the region was controlled by a powerful family of feudal lords. It is the cradle of the House of Plantagenet which ruled England from the twelfth century. During this time the Hospital of Saint-Jean was built in Angers by King Henry II of England. The edifice still stands to this day, now housing an important museum. In 1204 Angers was conquered by King Philippe II. The Huguenots took it in 1585, and the Vendean royalists were defeated nearby in 1793.

The site of a massive and ancient château, the city is also noted for the impressive twin spires of the twelfth century Cathedral of Saint-Maurice. Other noteworthy churches around Angers include St. Serge, an abbey-church of the 12th and 15th centuries, and the twelfth century La Trinité. The elaborately sculptured eleventh and twelfth century arcades of the famous abbey of Saint Aubin survive in the courtyard of the Prefecture and Hôtel du Departement. The tower of the abbey church has also survived nearby. Ruins of the old churches of Toussaint (13th century) and Notre-Dame du Ronçeray (11th century) are also nearby. The ancient hospital of St. Jean (12th century) is best known for its Jean Lurcat tapestries. The Logis Barrault, a mansion built in 1486-92, houses the Musee des Beaux-Arts, which has a large collection of paintings and sculptures. In 1984 the former abbey church of Toussaint became the Musee David d'Angers, containing works by the sculptor David d'Angers, who was a native of the town. Look out for his bronze statue (middle of a main boulevard near the museum) of René of Anjou who was born in the chateau of Angers.

The early prosperity of the town was largely due to the nearby quarries of slate, whose abundant use for the roofs of Angers led to the city's nickname, la ville noire. Other industries included the distillation of liqueurs from fruit (the orange liqueur Cointreau is only distilled in the town of Angers and the surrounding areas).

The Château d'Angers is on a rocky ridge overhanging the river Maine. In the 9th century, the fortress came under the authority of the powerful Counts of Anjou, becoming part of the Angevin empire of the Plantagenet Kings of England during the 12th century. In 1204, the region was conquered by Philip II and an enormous château was built by his grandson, Louis IX ("Saint Louis") in the early part of the 13th century. Nearly 600 m (2,000 ft) in circumference, and protected by seventeen massive towers, the walls of the château encompass 6.17 acres (25,000 m²). In 1352, John II le Bon, gave the château to his son, Louis I. Married to the daughter of the wealthy Duke of Brittany, Louis had the château modified,

and in 1373 commissioned the famous Apocalypse Tapestry from the painter Hennequin de Bruges and the Parisian tapestry-weaver Nicolas Bataille. Louis II added a chapel (1405–12) and royal apartments to the complex. The chapel is a sainte chapelle, the name given to churches which enshrined a relic of the Passion. In this case the relic was a splinter of the fragment of the True Cross which had been acquired by Louis IX. In the early 15th century, the hapless dauphin who, with the assistance of Joan of Arc would become King Charles VII, had to flee Paris and was given sanctuary at the château in Angers. In 1562, Catherine de Medici had the château restored as a powerful fortress, but, her son, Henry III, reduced the height of the towers. The chateau was severely damaged during World War II by the Nazis when a munitions storage dump inside the château exploded. Today, owned by the City of Angers, the massive, austere château has been converted to a museum housing the oldest and largest collection of medieval tapestries in the world, with the 14th century "Apocalypse Tapestry" as one of its priceless treasures.

St. Aubin Albinus, also known as Aubin, entered the monastery of Tincillac when a youth, was elected Abbot when he was thirty-five, and was named Bishop of Angers in 529. He was known for his generosity to the sick and the indigent, widows, and orphans; for his work in ransoming slaves, and for his holiness and the many miracles he is reputed to have performed both during his lifetime and after his death. His feast day is March 1.

Route Summary: the exit from Angers continues with an easy passage beside la Maine. Angers continues to be skirted using farm tracks and a zig-zag path through market gardens and orchards before following and then crossing the Loire and Louret on the busy N160 at les Ponts-de-Cé. The short section on the GR3 has obstacles for horse and bike riders, but an alternate is available. The path then heads south towards Brissac-Quincé on small roads and tracks through the vineyards. **Look out for:** * Ponts de Cé: Eglise Saint Maurille, 19th century church, built on the foundations of an 11th century church, and Pont Dumnacus (1846-1849)

Way Point	Distance	Directions	Verification Point	Compass
1		From Angers centre at the junction between Quai Robert Fèvre and Pont de Verdun, continue straight ahead with the river on the left	Across the river from Cathédrale Saint-Maurice d'Angers	SW
2	80	Bear left down the cobbled ramp towards the river-side. **Note:-** horse riders should remain on the road and turn right to Way Point #4	Red and yellow and GR signs	SW
3	170	Pass under low bridge		NW
4	80	Turn left and proceed along the river-side path		SW

Angers to Brissac-Quincé 26.6km

Way Point	Distance	Directions	Verification Point	Compass
5	3900	Continue straight ahead over the bridge		SW
6	700	Bear right up the ramp and turn left to cross the metal footbridge over the river Maine	Pont de Pruniers	E
7	700	Turn sharp right and take the track down the short hill turning left at the entrance to old railway tunnel	Wooden barrier and St James sign	S
8	500	Continue straight ahead through wooden barriers	Keep large old house to the left	S
9	600	Bear right through wooden barriers	St James sign	SW
10	600	After going through the wooden barriers bear left and pass under the railway bridge	St James and yellow stripe sign	SE
11	120	Immediately after the railway bridge turn right through the wooden barriers	Yellow stripe sign	SW
12	180	Turn left up a track passing between 2 large stones		E
13	150	Continue straight ahead on the road towards the T-junction	Factory Tolinov on the left and St James sign	SE
14	170	At the T-junction turn right on the D41	St James sign	S
15	50	Turn left between houses onto a minor road leading to a track	St James sign	E
16	200	Keep straight ahead with a line of trees on the left and market garden on the right		NE
17	150	Turn right on a broad track just before reaching greenhouses on the left	St James sign	SE
18	500	At junction with a minor road turn left on the road	St James sign	N
19	160	Turn right on a track between orchard on the left and hedgerow on the right	St James sign	E
20	300	At the end of the orchard, go straight ahead on a small bridge over a drainage pipe and turn left, leaving greenhouses behind	St James sign	N
21	120	Turn right keeping trees on the right	St James sign	SE
22	140	At T-junction in the track turn right towards the greenhouses	St James sign	S

Way Point	Distance	Directions	Verification Point	Compass
23	500	At the entrance to the market garden, cross the main road and take the track opposite	Chemin verger, St James sign	SE
24	40	At the junction with the road turn left on the road	St James sign and exit from les Hauts de Port Thibault	E
25	80	Turn right on chemin de la Vanrie	St James sign	S
26	160	At T-junction with a major road turn left, route de Bouchemaine	St James sign	NE
27	300	Turn right keeping industrial buildings on the left. **Note:-** horses are prohibited on the path ahead at weekends and on bank holidays. An alternate route is possible by continuing on route de Bouchemain, turning right on rue du Cormier and bearing left on rue de l'Authion until reaching the bridge at Way Point #37	St James sign	S
28	200	Pass through wooden barriers and turn left with the river Loire on the right and a wall on the left		E
29	700	Continue straight ahead in the direction of l'Authion	River remaining on the right	NE
30	200	With a road to the left continue straight ahead across the park keeping parallel to the river		NE
31	600	Beside the river bridge cross the road and continue straight ahead on the gravel track with the narrow waterway on the right		NE
32	2000	At the crossroads turn right on rue David d'Angers, D160 (formerly N160)	Cross the river bridge over l'Authion	S
33	700	At the roundabout continue straight ahead in the direction of Brissac-Quincé		S
34	1700	After crossing the bridge over the Louet, turn left through a gap in the wall and down steps. **Note:-** horse-riders should continue on the road and take the next road (D132) on the left and rejoin the main route at Way Point #37	GR and St James signs opposite the hotel le Bosquet sign	NE
35	200	Take the right fork	GR sign	E
36	300	At T-junction in tracks turn right	GR sign	S

Angers to Brissac-Quincé 26.6km

Way Point	Distance	Directions	Verification Point	Compass
37	170	At a T-junction with a main road turn left	GR sign	E
38	300	Bear right onto a dirt track	St James sign	SE
39	800	Bear left under the road bridge	GR sign	NE
40	190	Bear right on the gravel track away from the highway		E
41	150	At the crossroads in the track, turn right towards the water tower, leaving the GR to the left	St James sign on post on the left in the hedge before the junction	SE
42	600	At the junction with the main road cross over and take chemin du Champ Vallée	St James sign	SE
43	400	At the crossroads continue straight ahead on chemin du Champ Vallée		SE
44	300	At the crossroads continue straight ahead on chemin du Champ Vallée		S
45	500	At the crossroads continue straight ahead on chemin de l'Etang	St James sign, house no. 25 on the left	SE
46	300	Fork right onto a gravel track	St James sign	SE
47	150	At crossroads in the track continue straight ahead		SE
48	600	Cross the minor road and continue on the track	St James sign, white house no. 58 on the left	SE
49	400	Cross the minor road and continue on the gravel track	Pond on the left	SE
50	900	At crossroads continue straight ahead on chemin des Grands Champs	St James sign	SE
51	300	At crossroads in the track continue straight ahead on the gravel track between 2 houses	St James sign	SE
52	200	At the crossroads turn right on the road	St James sign	S
53	500	At the roundabout take the second exit in the direction of Brissac-Quincé		SW
54	180	At the second roundabout take the fourth exit direction l'Homois Clabeau		SE
55	100	Turn left direction l'Homois	St James sign	SE

Angers to Brissac-Quincé 26.6km

Way Point	Distance	Directions	Verification Point	Compass
56	500	Turn right direction la Haute Bâte	St James sign	SE
57	1300	At junction with a minor road turn left up the hill, rue Pierre Niveleau	St James sign	SE
58	300	At T-junction turn right on rue de Verdun	St James sign	S
59	200	Arrive in Brissac-Quincé beside the entrance to the church of Saint Vincent		

Useful Contacts

Tourist Offices

Office de Tourisme , 8 pl République 49320 BRISSAC QUINCE
Tel: 0033 (0)2 41 91 21 50

Doctor

Voineau Hervé, 7 pl Gén de Gaulle 49320 BRISSAC QUINCE
Tel: 0033 (0)2 41 91 24 53

Veterinary

Bourcier François, 34 Bis pl Georges Clémenceau 49320 BRISSAC QUINCE
Tel: 0033 (0)2 41 91 20 91

Farrier

Geray Pascal, Les Justeries chem Landes 49800 TRELAZE   Tel: 0033 (0)2 41 34 12 15

Angers to Brissac-Quincé 26.6km

Accommodation - Hotel/B&B	Price	Opening	Animals
Gripon Olivier, 4 rte Hutreau 49130 SAINTE GEMMES SUR LOIRE Tel: 0033 (0)2 41 79 20 52	B2	All Year	🐎
Le Ponceau, rte du Hutreau 49130 SAINTE GEMMES SUR LOIRE Tel: 0033 (0)2 41 44 62 05	B2	All Year	🐎
Hôtel Restaurant Le Bosquet, 2 r Maurice Berne 49130 LES PONTS DE CÉ Tel: 0033 (0)2 41 57 72 42	B3	All Year	🐎
Le Relais de Cé, 18 r David d'Angers 49130 LES PONTS DE CÉ Tel: 0033 (0)2 41 44 87 47	B2	All Year	🐎
Hôtel Première Classe, ZA Moulin Marcille 22 r Paul Pousset LES 49130 PONTS DE CE Tel: 0033 (0) 800 0 805	B2	All Year	🐎
Hôtel Boucherie, 22 r Paul Pousset 49130 LES PONTS DE CE Tel: 0033 (0)2 41 69 42 63		All Year	🐎
Bagatelle Prim'Hôtel, Zac du Moulin Marcille 20 rue Paul Pousset LES 49130 PONTS DE CÉ Tel: 0033 (0)2 41 69 76 97	B2	All Year	🐎
Moulin De Clabeau, 49320 Brissac Quincé Tel: 0033 (0)2 41 91 22 09	B2	All Year	🐎
La Demeure du Goupil, Le Goupil 49320 BRISSAC QUINCÉ Tel: 0033 (0)2 41 66 62 40 contact@demeure-du-goupil.com	B3	All Year	🐎

Hostel	Price	Opening	Animals
Maison Familiale CFA, 51 R Louis Moron 49320 BRISSAC QUINCE Tel: 0033 (0)2 41 91 23 25	B1	All Year	🐎

Camping	Price	Opening	Animals
Camping de l'Ile du Château, Avenue de la Boire Salée - 49130 LES PONTS DE CÉ Tel: 0033 (0)2 41 44 62 05	B1	01/05 - 01/09	🐎
Camping de l'Ile du Château, Pontonnier, Avenue de la boire salée 49130 LES PONTS-DE-CÉ Tel: 0033 (0)2 41 44 62 05	B1	01/04 - 31/10	🐎
Les Varennes, Parc les Varennes 49610 MURS ERIGNE Tel: 0033 (0)2 41 57 82 15	B1	All Year	🐎
CESBRON, domaine Etang 49320 BRISSAC QUINCE Tel: 0033 (0)9 62 01 44 64	B1	All Year	🐎
Camping Caravaning du Domaine de l'Etang, domaine Etang 49320 BRISSAC QUINCE Tel: 0033 (0)2 41 91 70 61	B1	All Year	🐎

Equestrian Centre

Ecurie de Cé, 64 Bis rte de Sorges 49130 LES PONTS DE CÉ
Tel: 0033 (0)2 41 34 16 69 **Note:** 5.7km from Sainte Gemmes sure Loire

The **Château de Brissac** was originally built as a fortified castle by the Counts of Anjou in the 11th century. In the 15th century, the structure was rebuilt by Pierre de Brézé, a wealthy chief minister to King Charles VII. During the French Wars of Religion, Château Brissac was made a possession in 1589 by the Protestant, Henri of Navarre. Severely damaged, the fortress was scheduled to be demolished. However, Charles II de Cossé sided with Henri of Navarre who soon was crowned King of France. In gratitude, King Henri gave him the property, the title Duc de Brissac and the money to rebuild the chateau in 1611. Its construction made it the highest château in France, its façade reflecting the influences of that century's Baroque architecture. Through marriage, the Cossé-Brissac family also acquired the Château Montreuil-Bellay but later sold it. The descendants of the Duc de Brissac maintained the château until 1792 when the property was ransacked during the Revolution. It remained in this condition until a restoration program began in 1844, which was carried on during the 19th century by the Duke's descendants. Today, the Château Brissac is still owned by a de Cossé family member. It has seven storeys altogether, making it the tallest chateau in the Loire Valley. The chateau is open to tours and its luxurious gilded theatre hosts the annual Val de Loire festival.

The Benedictine Abbey of St Aubin in Angers ruled over the parish from 769. In 1496, the parishioners undertook to enlarge the church, building a choir with gothic vaults (higher to avoid the frequent floods), and a second narrower knave to the North, with a three-sided gable. Since then **St Aubin church** has been the subject of attack and destruction. First by the Calvinists in 1562, then during the Revolution and finally sustaining bomb damage in 1944. Tragically, just as the restoration of the original beams was coming to an end, the church was burnt down to the ground. Nevertheless, the now restored church has been back in use since December 1984.

Angers to Brissac-Quincé 26.6km

Le Priuré, les Alleuds

Crucifix, displaying St James scallop shell and pilgrim staff

Originally the term 'troglodyte' comes from the Greek term for a cave dweller. Away from the Loire, where the cliffs lend themselves to the troglodyte dwellings, troglodyte villages were built by digging holes like large craters and then carving out the walls. The best example is at **Rochemenier** and the museum reveals a community of two ancient farms and their associated dwellings which have been carved out of the local stone in a quarry type setting. There are barns, a wine cellar, the all important communal village oven, stables and even an amazing underground Church to visit. Guided tours available. Open April- October, daily 09.30-12.00 and 14.00-19.00).

Route Summary: this is an undemanding section taking minor roads and broad farm tracks at a safe distance from the parallel and busy D761. **Look out for:** Noyant La Plaine - St Jacques crucifix displaying pilgrim staff and St James scallop shell.

Way Point	Distance	Directions	Verification Point	Compass
1		From the entrance to the church in Brissac-Quincé turn left, keeping the church on the left, and proceed along rue de Verdun		S
2	120	Continue straight ahead down the hill with the château on the right	Place de Tertre	SE
3	300	Turn right onto via Caluso towards large park gates	St James sign	SW
4	110	Just in front of the gates turn left onto rue Duchesse		SE

Way Point	Distance	Directions	Verification Point	Compass
5	90	Opposite house no. 11, turn right onto a gravel track	St James sign	S
6	200	At the top of the hill bear right on rue Georges Pompidou	St James sign	S
7	180	At the mini roundabout bear left remaining on rue Georges Pompidou	St James sign, house on the right with fine gardens and member of ASPEJA	E
8	120	At T-junction turn right on rue Raphaël Lecuit		S
9	1600	At the crossroads with the D748 cross straight over in the direction of la Belle Etoile	St James sign	SE
10	400	Bear right onto the gravel track beside the stone cross	St James sign	S
11	400	At crossroads in the track turn left	St James sign	E
12	1200	At T-junction turn right and continue straight ahead over the crossroads, keeping the Vert Anjou granary on the right	St James sign	S
13	300	Continue straight ahead in the direction of Sablière des Grands Biousses		S
14	500	At the crossroads continue straight ahead ignoring the sign to Sablière des Grands Biousses	St James sign	SE
15	200	At the T-junction turn left into the village of les Alleuds	St James sign	NE
16	300	Turn right onto rue du Prieuré	St James sign, crucifix to the left	SE
17	200	Bear right with a pond on your right and the church on your left		S
18	90	At T-junction turn right on rue du Layon	St James sign	SW
19	400	Turn left onto a gravel track beside the stream	St James sign	SE
20	900	At junction keep right with a house to your left		SE
21	150	At fork in the track bear left	St James sign	SE
22	300	At junction keep right towards a band of trees		SE
23	200	At junction go straight ahead keeping trees to your right		SE
24	700	At crossroads in the tracks go straight ahead towards the church keeping trees to the left		SE

Brissac-Quincé to Rochemenier 24.5km

Way Point	Distance	Directions	Verification Point	Compass
25	500	Cross over the minor road and continue on the track towards the village of Saulgé-l'Hôpital		SE
26	200	Continue straight ahead on the path keeping old farm buildings to the left		SE
27	150	At T-junction in the track turn right towards small château		SE
28	400	At the junction with the D176 go straight ahead to take the small tarmac road opposite	St James and la Commanderie signs	SE
29	170	Bear right from the gravel track onto a grass track beside the hedge		S
30	170	At junction with a gravel track bear left		SE
31	130	At T-junction in the track turn right		S
32	90	Bear left on the track		SE
33	700	At junction in the track turn right. **Note**:- at the time of writing there is a large road construction to the left, which may change the routing of the path. In the event of changes keep parallel to the main road on the left until reaching the village of Noyant-la-Plaine		SW
34	110	Turn left remaining on the track	Parallel to main road	SE
35	700	At T-junction turn left and immediately right before the 150m sign		SE
36	400	At T-junction turn left and immediately right before the 100m sign with orchards on the right	St James sign	SE
37	300	At junction turn left towards the main road		E
38	150	At the crossroads with the main road, cross straight over onto the D70 direction Gennes		E
39	130	At crossroads turn right on the Voie Napoléon	St James sign	SE
40	200	At crossroads go straight ahead remaining on Voie Napoléon. **Note**:- St James cross on the left	St James sign	SE
41	700	At T-junction turn right	Line of trees ahead	SE
42	1000	At the fork in the village of Ambillou-Château bear left beside house no. 7, on rue de la Besnardière	St James sign	E

Brissac-Quincé to Rochemenier 24.5km

Way Point	Distance	Directions	Verification Point	Compass
43	170	At T-junction with route de Saune, turn right and then immediately left on rue de la Fontaine	St James sign	E
44	900	Approximately 70m after passing through the tunnel under the major road turn left on the track		N
45	180	At T-junction in the track turn right	St James sign on wooden post	NE
46	400	At junction with a minor road turn right and then immediately left onto a further track	St James sign	E
47	500	At junction with a minor road turn right		SE
48	130	At junction turn right and then immediately left beside the greenhouses		SE
49	400	Turn left towards the ponds		E
50	600	At the T-junction turn left and follow the track uphill towards the village of la Bournée		E
51	600	At the road junction continue straight ahead into la Bournée		S
52	80	Turn left to leave rue du Lavoir	St James sign	NE
53	300	At the crossroads turn right onto rue du Polissoir		SE
54	300	At the crossroads in the village go straight ahead on the C6, route de Villeneuve	Direction Dénezé	SE
55	500	Turn right direction Dénezé		SE
56	700	Turn right onto a track following the red and white GR signs		SW
57	700	At T-junction in the track turn left	GR sign	E
58	300	At junction with a minor road turn right		S
59	200	Turn left direction Moulin Gouré	St James sign	E
60	400	Turn right into les Patauderies	St James sign	S
61	140	Continue straight ahead onto a grass track	GR sign	S

Brissac-Quincé to Rochemenier 24.5km

Way Point	Distance	Directions	Verification Point	Compass
62	600	At junction with a gravel track turn right	Towards the village of Rochemenier	SW
63	600	Turn right towards the village centre	St James and GR signs	W
64	130	At crossroads with the D177 go straight ahead	St James and GR signs	W
65	300	At fork keep left		SW
66	140	At the crossroads turn left towards the church		SE
67	80	Arrive in Rochemenier centre beside the church		

Accommodation - Hotel / B&B	Price	Opening	Animals
De Rocquigny Marie Helene, Aligny Nord La Cotiniére 49320 GREZILLE Tel: 0033 (0)2 41 59 72 21 **Note:** 3.5km from Saulgé-l'Hôpital,	B2	All Year	
Maryse et Jean-Marie COCANDEAU, 16 route de Grenet- La Grézille 49700 AMBILLOU-CHATEAU Tel: 0033 (0)2 41 5 94 84 Mobile: 0033 (0)6 82 38 91 31 www.symphoniederoses.monsite.orange.fr	B3	All Year	
Les Délices de la Roche, 16 rue du Musée 49700 LOURESSE-ROCHEMENIER Tel: 0033 (0)2 41 50 15 26 Mobile: 0033 (0)6 89 51 69 47 www.delicesdelaroche.com accueil@delicesdelaroche.com	B2	All Year	

Hostel	Price	Opening	Animals
Gite d'etape l'Ecuyer de la Paumelière, 2 rue Paumelière 49320 SALUGÉ L'HOPITAL Tel: 0033 (0)2 41 45 52 26	B1	All Year	
Troglo Gîtes / gîte d'étape, 3 rue des Troglogîtes 49700 LOURESSE-ROCHEMENIER Tel: 0033 (02 41 59 07 02 www.troglogite.com chauvinb@aol.com	B1	All Year	

Equestrian Centre

Les Ecuries Verrinoises, 9 r Caves 49400 VERRIE
Tel: 0033 (0)2 41 38 08 89 **Note:** 6km from Louresse-Rochemenier

Brissac-Quincé to Rochemenier 24.5km

Useful Contacts

Tourist Offices

Office de Tourisme du Saumurois, pl Concorde 49260 MONTREUIL BELLAY
Tel: 0033 (0)2 41 52 32 39

Doctor

Michenaud Bernard, 336 r Estienvrin 49260 MONTREUIL BELLAY
Tel: 0033 (0)2 41 52 37 80   Mobile: 0033 (0)9 61 27 02 30

Veterinary

Piquet Hélène, 26 rte Méron 49260 MONTREUIL BELLAY
Tel: 0033 (0)2 41 50 95 15   Mobile: 0033 (0)9 60 19 15 36

Farrier

Reynald Gorry, Puyraveau 19 r Puy de L'Ormeau 79100 SAINT LEGER DE MONTBRUN
Mobile: 0033 (0)6 62 04 79 36

Ruins of Collegial St Denis built 1472 until 1484

The property, **Montreuil-Bellay**, consisting of more than 1,000 acres (4 km²), was acquired by a Bellay family member in 1025 but was seized by a Plantagenet during the second half of the 1100s. After the defeat of the English by King Philippe II, a Bellay descendant, Guillaume de Melun, had high, massive, walls constructed including 13 interlocking towers, with entry only via a fortified gateway. During the French Wars of Religion (1562-1598) the town of Montreuil-Bellay was ransacked and burned but the sturdy fortress suffered little damage. Ownership of the castle changed several times but during the French Revolution the castle was seized by the revolutionary government and used as a prison for women suspected of being royalists. The Chateau is now used for premium wine making.

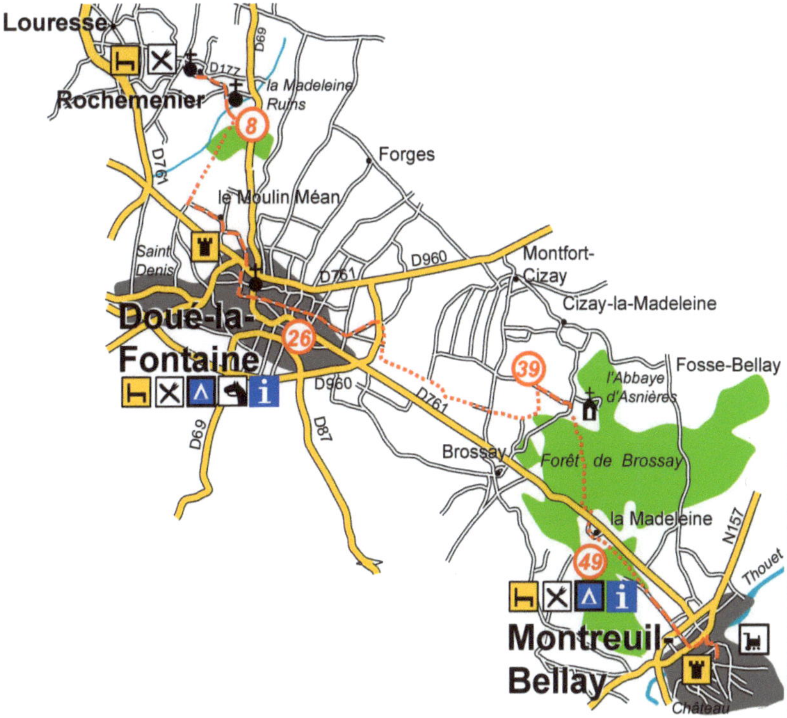

Route Summary: this shorter section is generally undertaken on farm tracks. The key feature is the zig-zag transit of Doué-la-Fontaine. In the event of difficulties make your way to the Centre les Perrières — Way Point #26, from where the town exit is straight forward

Way Point	Distance	Directions	Verification Point	Compass
1		From the church in Rochemenier turn left and follow rue du Musée	Church on the left, museum on the right	E
2	300	Continue straight ahead on the D177 direction Dénezé		E
3	300	Turn right in the direction of Varanne	St James sign	SE
4	500	Continue straight ahead onto a smaller road with farm buidings (Varanne) on the left	St James sign	SE
5	150	Take the right fork keeping the ruins of la Madeleine to the left		SW
6	70	Bear left on the track chemin du Boassard		S
7	200	Continue over the stream following the track as it turns quickly right and left towards edge of the woods		SE
8	200	Turn right onto the long straight forest track, Grande Allée		SW
9	1000	Continue straight ahead on the road	Long low white building on the left	SW
10	800	At the crossroads turn left towards houses – les Blanchisseries	St James sign	SE
11	800	At a fork in the road bear right towards a water tower	Pass sports complex on the left	SE
12	1100	At a T-junction with a major road (D761) turn right		W
13	40	At the zebra crossing turn left onto the tarmac pathway		S
14	200	At the junction with the road, rue Albert Camus, beat left		SW
15	70	At the crossroads go straight ahead following the signs for the ruins of Saint Denis		S
16	200	Beside the ruins turn left on rue Saint Denis		E
17	160	At a T-junction with a main road cross straight over towards the church		SE
18	40	With the church to your left, bear left up the hill, rue Saint Pierre		SE

Rochemenier to Montreuil-Bellay 21.4km

Way Point	Distance	Directions	Verification Point	Compass
19	50	Bear right down the narrow street – Petite rue Saint Pierre		S
20	60	At the crossroads turn left on rue du Commerce		E
21	140	At the roundabout take the first exit to the right direction place Renée Nicolas	St James sign	SE
22	100	Turn left onto rue du Petit Bois		E
23	300	At a mini-roundabout bear right	Rue des Récollets	SE
24	60	Turn left on rue des Perrières	Keep church to the left	E
25	300	At the crossroads continue straight ahead direction les Perrières		E
26	300	Having passed beside the centre de les Perrières continue straight ahead on rue des Perrières		SE
27	100	At the T-junction turn left and immediately right onto chemin des Varennes		SE
28	700	At the crossroads continue straight ahead	St James sign	SE
29	140	Turn left onto rue de Montfort	Troglodyte restaurant on the right	NE
30	500	At the roundabout go straight ahead and pass under the road bridge		E
31	200	Shortly after passing under the road turn right onto a gravel track		S
32	500	Turn right on the gravel track to remain parallel with the main road	St James sign	S
33	300	Turn left in front of 2 large stones		SE
34	800	Continue straight ahead on the tarmac road		SE
35	200	Continue straight ahead on the track towards the trees		SE
36	1000	Continue straight ahead with wall to the right		E
37	500	At a crossroads with the D174, continue straight ahead direction le Vauboureau	St James sign and la Croix du Vauboureau	E

Rochemenier to Montreuil-Bellay 21.4km

Way Point	Distance	Directions	Verification Point	Compass
38	700	At T-junction turn left	Pass farm, la Broise, on the right	N
39	900	At junction turn right towards l'Abbaye d'Asnières		SE
40	800	At the entrance to l'Abbaye d'Asnières turn right		S
41	130	Bear left onto a grass track beside iron gates	Blue and yellow stripe sign on tree	SE
42	200	Bear right following the blue stripe sign		S
43	200	Take the left fork following the blue stripe		S
44	200	At crossroads in the tracks go straight ahead	Blue stripe	S
45	500	At crossroads in the tracks go straight ahead	Blue stripe	S
46	900	Just before the main road turn left onto the track that runs parallel to the road	Blue stripe and St James sign	SE
47	200	Turn right towards the main road		S
48	60	Cross the D761 and take rue du Pieuré	St James sign	S
49	400	Pass la Madeleine on the left and bear right onto a gravel track running parallel to the main road		SE
50	400	Continue straight ahead	Blue stripe	SE
51	80	Continue straight ahead	Blue stripe	SE
52	500	At crossroads in the tracks go straight ahead in the direction of Montreuil-Bellay		SE
53	1400	Continue straight ahead towards the town	St James sign	SE
54	600	At the junction turn left onto avenue Paul Painlevé. **Note:-** the next section will return to this point at Way Point #04. If you wish to bypass Montreuil Bellay cross the road to follow the St James sign opposite.	Keep the river, le Thouet, on the right	NE
55	300	At the T-junction turn right direction Poitiers	Cross the river bridge	SE
56	300	Turn right on rue des Douves	Signs for chambre d'hôte and Hôtel Splendid	S
57	200	Arrive in Montreuil-Bellay centre beside the entrance to the château		

Accommodation Hotel/ B&B	Price	Opening	Animals
Logis de France Auberge, 104 r Cholet 49700 DOUÉ LA FONTAINE Tel: 0033 (0)2 41 59 22 44	B3	All Year	🐴
Au Chais de Taunay, 17 r Alger 49700 DOUE LA FONTAINE Tel: 0033 (0)2 41 83 09 54	B2	All Year	🐴
Mme Penet, 13 rue des Arénes 49700 DOUE LA FONTAINE Tel: 0033 (0)2 41 59 72 30	B2	All Year	
Mme dout, 34 rue de Soulanger 49700 DOUE LA FONTAINE Tel: 0033 (0)2 41 59 21 43	B2	All Year	🐴
Les Murets de Trézé, les Murets 115 r Société 49260 MONTREUIL BELLAY Tel: 0033 (0)2 41 50 84 85 les-murets-de-treze@wanadoo.fr www.murets.com/index.html	B3	All Year	🐴
Hôtel le Splendid, 139 r Doct Gaudrez 49260 MONTREUIL BELLAY Tel: 0033: (0)2 41 53 10 00	B2	All Year	🐴
Hôtellerie Billy, 96 r Nationale 49260 MONTREUIL BELLAY Tel: 0033 (0)2 41 53 10 10	B2	All Year	🐴
PR Guezenec Monique, 321 r Nationale 49260 MONTREUIL BELLAY Tel: 0033 (0)2 41 52 33 88	B2	All Year	🐴
Mercier Liliane, 115 r Société 49260 MONTREUIL BELLAY Tel: 0033 (0)9 79 65 66 23	B2	All Year	🐴
Boulay Daniel, 393 r Nationale 49260 MONTREUIL BELLAY Tel: 0033 (0)2 41 52 44 99	B2	All Year	
Fleming Julie, 267 r Laveau 49260 MONTREUIL BELLAY Tel: 0033 (0)2 41 51 13 28	B2	All Year	🐴
Mme Claudie Bernay, 42 Place du Marché, 49260 MONTREUIL BELLAY Tel: 0033 (0)2 42 38 86 98	B2	All Year	🐴
Hostel	**Price**	**Opening**	**Animals**
Maison Familale Rurale, 22 rue Jean Mermoz 49700 DOUE LA FONTAINE Tel: 0033 (0)241 59 14 47	B1	All Year	🐴
Camping	**Price**	**Opening**	**Animals**
Camping Municipal, r des Blanchisseries 49700 DOUÉ LA FONTAINE Tel: 0033 (0)2 41 59 14 47	B1	All Year	🐴
Les Nobis, rue du Georges Girouy 49700 DOUÉ LA FONTAINE Tel: 0033 (0)2 41 52 33 66	B1	All Year	🐴
Equestrian Centre			

La Chevallerie, rte de Blanchesseries, 49700 DOUE LA FONTAINE
Tel: 0033 (0)2 41 59 90 82

Rochemenier to Montreuil-Bellay 21.4km

Scallop shell detail on Eglise Collégiale Notre-Dame, Le Puy Notre Dame

Eglise Collégiale Notre-Dame, Le Puy Notre Dame

The inhabitants of **Thouars** are known as les Thouarsais and les Thouarsaises. The town was the birthplace of the medieval general Louis de La Trémoille. In 1619 his heir Henri de La Trémoille married Marie de la Tour d'Auvergne, sister of Turenne, who razed the old gothic château-fort to build the present château, which was designed by Jacques Lemercier and completed in the brief space of three years, 1635–1638. Its main façade is more than 110 m. The Trémoilles were dispossessed at the Revolution and the château became a barracks and later a prison. It has been restored for its present use as a school. The adjoining Sainte-Chapelle dating from the early 16th century is Gothic in style with Renaissance details, and was built by Gabrielle de Bourbon, wife of Louis I. of La Tremoille. The church of St Medard, rebuilt in the 15th century, preserves a doorway of a previous Romanesque building, while the church of St Laon (12th and 15th centuries) was formerly attached to an abbey which now serves as the town-hall. It has a fine square tower in the Romanesque style and contains the sculptured tomb of the abbot Nicholas. Remains of the ramparts of the town dating from the 13th century and flanked by huge towers are still to be seen. A bridge of the same period crosses the river Thouet, which runs through the town.

Thouars Château on the banks of the Thouet

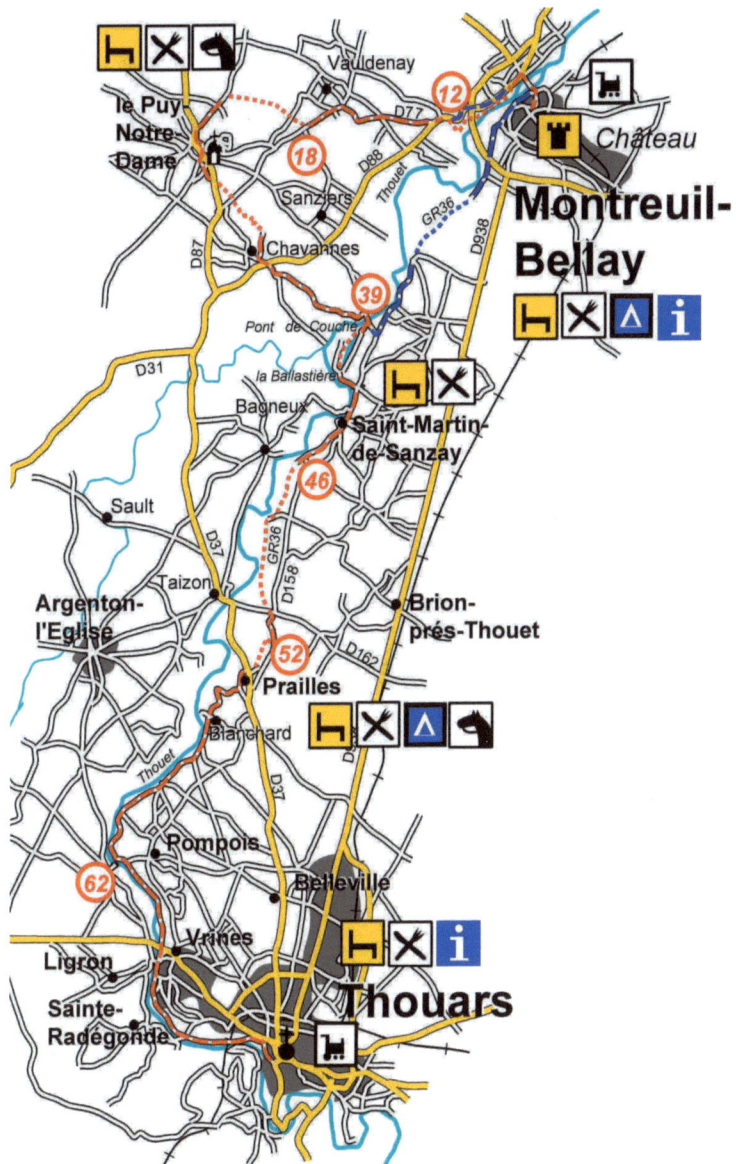

Route Summary: this is a long section with limited opportunities for accommodation before Thouars. The alternate route reduces the journey considerably by bypassing le Puy-Notre-Dame. The latter half of the section (and the alternate route) follow the GR 36, leaving behind the excellent St James signs but gaining the generally good red and white signs of the Fédération Français de la Randonnée Pédestres - FFRP. There are long stretches on minor roads making use of the regional cycle network. **Look out for:** * Le Puy Notre Dame - The Holy Belt of the Virgin preserved in the Collegial.

Way Point	Distance	Directions	Verification Point	Compass
1		From the entrance to the château turn left to return down the hill along rue des Douves		N
2	200	At the T-junction turn left in the direction of domaine des Garennes. **Note:-** the signed route progresses via the historic village of le Puy-Notre-Dame however it is possible to bypass the village and reduce the section by 8 km by following the GR 36 (the red and white striped signs) from the left turn just before the river bridge to Way Point #39 at Pont de Couché. The GR 36 follows minor roads and farms tracks keeping the river Thouet to the right.		NW
3	300	Turn left direction Vaudelnay		SW
4	300	Turn left onto impasse des Isles. **Note:- 1.** This is the point where the section starts for those who have chosen to bypass Montreuil-Bellay. **2.** The path ahead includes narrow and weak wooden bridges that are unsuitable for horses. Riders should remain on the road to pass under the ring road and rejoin the main route at Way Point #12	St James sign	SE
5	110	Bear right on the grass track with the river to your left		SW
6	500	Continue across small wooden bridge		SW
7	400	Bear right to leave the river and pass through a gap in the wire fence and take the tunnel under the ring road		SW
8	170	Bear right on the faint path up a small rise		NW
9	70	At the top of the rise bear left towards a metal gate		SW
10	40	Continue through the metal gate		SW
11	130	At a T-junction in the track turn right	St James sign	NW
12	300	At junction with road, turn left on the D77 towards Vauldenay. **Note:-** riders rejoin at this point		W
13	1400	At the crossroads beside the statue, la Bonne Dame, take the second left		W
14	190	At the crossroads continue straight ahead towards le Moulin de Batereau	Blue stripe and St James sign	W
15	700	At the T-junction turn left	St James sign	SW

Montreuil-Bellay to Thouars 32.8km

Way Point	Distance	Directions	Verification Point	Compass
16	90	Continue straight ahead. **Note:-** the signed route turns left down rue Saint Pierre la Casse, but adds 500m with no advantage, returning to the road at the next Way Point.	St James sign	SW
17	400	Continue straight ahead on the road	Blue stripe sign	SW
18	300	Turn right onto a gravel track between the vines just before the sign to Sanziers	Blue stripe and St James sign	NW
19	400	At junction with a minor road continue straight ahead on the track		W
20	1500	At junction with a minor road turn left towards the village of le Puy-Notre-Dame		SW
21	800	At T-junction turn left into the centre of the village		S
22	90	Turn left just before the Centre Ville sign	Rue des Picards	SE
23	300	Turn right towards place du Champ de Mars and the church	Rue de l'Eperon	SW
24	110	Bear left on rue de la Collégialle		S
25	30	Turn right on rue de Sainte	St James sign	SW
26	110	Turn left on rue de la Cour Nault	St James sign	SE
27	70	Turn right onto rue de la Jalterie		S
28	90	Turn left in front of a house with large iron gates and immediately right		S
29	90	Turn left in front of house no. 10	Blue and yellow sign	SE
30	180	At road junction, cross straight over onto rue Saint Nicolas	Stone crucifix on the right, St James sign	SE
31	600	At junction with a minor road continue straight ahead on the track	Blue and yellow sign	SE
32	900	At a T-junction in the tracks turn right towards the hamlet of Chavannes		S
33	200	Continue straight ahead on rue l'Arguray	Blue stripe sign	S
34	200	Bear left just after château de Chavannes	St James sign	S
35	150	At the crossroads turn left on rue des Deux Croix		E

Montreuil-Bellay to Thouars 32.8km

Way Point	Distance	Directions	Verification Point	Compass
36	80	At junction turn left (on the D88) and immediately right in the direction le Coteau	St James sign	SE
37	300	Take the left fork direction le Coteau		SE
38	2000	At the T-junction turn right over the bridge		S
39	300	Just after crossing the bridge turn right direction la Ballastière. **Note:**- this is the end of the St James signing until reaching the village of Villedieu. The route will follow the GR36	GR sign	SW
40	100	Road forks continue straight ahead with the football pitch on the left	GR sign	SW
41	140	Turn right and then left keeping the lake on the left	GR sign	SW
42	800	At a T-junction turn left	GR sign	SE
43	600	At crossroads turn right direction Saint-Martin-de-Sanzay	GR sign	S
44	400	At mini-roundabout continue straight ahead into the village	GR sign and bridge to the right	SW
45	400	Turn right beside the bar au Bon Accueil and then take the first turning on the left, route de Compostelle	GR sign	SW
46	900	Fork right off the road onto an unmade track with the river directly on the right		SW
47	1300	At a crossroads in the track turn right into the trees	GR sign	W
48	120	Take the left fork	GR sign	S
49	300	Continue straight ahead with a line of trees on the left		S
50	500	At the junction keep straight ahead on the grassier track		S
51	1000	At crossroads go straight ahead direction Prailles	GR sign	S
52	600	Turn right onto a grass track between trees	GR sign	NW
53	180	Just before entering the woods turn left towards the farm		SW
54	600	At the T-junction turn right towards the village - Prailles	GR sign	W
55	100	At the crossroads go straight ahead in the direction of la Gennaire, route de la Chapelle	GR sign	W

Montreuil-Bellay to Thouars 32.8km

Way Point	Distance	Directions	Verification Point	Compass
56	90	At the T-junction turn left onto route de Tilleuf	GR sign and chapel on the right	S
57	300	At junction turn right	GR sign and walls to château	W
58	60	Roads forks, take the right fork keeping rue de la Fontaine to the left	GR sign	SW
59	1000	Continue straight ahead into the hamlet	GR sign	SW
60	120	Take the right fork with the river on the right, direction Moulin de Champigny	GR sign	SW
61	1200	Turn right direction le Moulin d'Enterré	GR sign	SW
62	1700	Take the right fork onto rue des Bas Coteaux	GR sign	SE
63	1700	Remain on the road bearing right on chemin de Enterré		S
64	400	Bear right down the hill with a hotel on the left	Footbridge to the right	S
65	1700	Continue straight ahead following the signs for the Thouars cycle route	GR sign	E
66	1800	At the top of the steep hill, rue de la Grande Côte Crevant, turn right		S
67	110	Continue straight ahead on rue Drouyneau de Brie		S
68	300	Continue straight ahead on rue Regnier Desmarais	GR sign	SE
69	140	Continue straight ahead on rue de Hôtel de Ville		SE
70	50	Arrive in Thouars centre beside the church of Saint Médard		

Montreuil-Bellay to Thouars 32.8km

Montreuil-Bellay to Thouars 32.8km

Accommodation Hotel/ B&B	Price	Opening	Animals
Le Chai de la Paleine, 10 pl Jules Raimbault 49260 PUY NOTRE DAME (LE) Tel: 0033 (0)2 41 38 28 25 lapaleine@wanadoo.fr	B2	All Year	🐴
AU MANOIR DE LA TÊTE ROUGE, 3 Place Jules Raimbault 49260 PUY NOTRE DAME (LE) Tel : 0033 (0)2 41 38 76 43	B3	All Year	🐴
Château Tour Grise, 1 rue des Ducs d'Aquitaine 49260 PUY NOTRE DAME (LE) Tel: 0033 (0)2 41 38 82 42	B2	All Year	🐴
Les Clos des Guyons, 6 rue du Moulin 49260 PUY NOTRE DAME (LE) Tel: 0033 (0)2 41 40 36 84	B2	All Year	🐴
L'Amandier, 20 rue de la Mairie 49260 PUY NOTRE DAME (LE) Tel: 0033 (0)2 41 67 59 77	B3	All Year	🐴
La Pinsonniére, 225 rue du Château à Sanziers 49260 PUY NOTRE DAME (LE) Tel: 0033 (0)2 41 59 12 95	B2	All Year	🐴
Alaine JACQUET, Imp de la Chapelle-Passay 79290 SAINT MARTIN DE SANZAY	B2	All Year	🐴
Acacia, 1 imp Gaston Chérau 79100 THOUARS Tel: 0033 (0)5 49 96 20 80	B2	All Year	🐴
PR Hôtel de la Gare, 1 pl Gare 79100 THOUARS Tel: 0033 (0)5 49 66 20 75 thouarshoteldelagare@wanadoo.fr	B2	All Year	🐴
Restaurant Hôtel Le Dauphin, 39 bd Pierre Curie 79100 THOUARS Tel: 0033 (0)5 49 66 02 26	B2	All Year	🐴
Roselyne CHARRUAULT, 12 rue du Vicomte 79100 THOUARS Tel: 0033 (0)5 49 66 03 78	B2	All Year	🐴

Hostel	Price	Opening	Animals
Mme Marcel Biguet, 5 place Jules Raimbault 49260 PUY NOTRE DAME (LE) Tel: 0033 (0)2 41 52 26 68 **Note:** for Groups	B1	All Year	🐴

Camping	Price	Opening	Animals
Camp Municipal Le Lambon 79370 PRAILLES Tel: 0033 (0)5 49 32 85 11	B1	All Year	

Equestrian Centre

Equi-Libre, 2 all Varenne 49260 SAINT MACAIRE DU BOIS
Tel: 0033 (0)2 41 50 95 40 **Note:** 2.95km from Le Puy Notre Dame

Relais Equestre de l'Hermitain, Bois Pineau 79800 SOUVIGNÉ
Tel: 0033 (0)5 49 06 99 01 **Note:** 3km from Prailles

Baudouin David, Lussaudiere 79370 Prailles Mobile: 0033 (0)6 11 30 88 18
ecuries.de.lussaudiere@club-internet.fr

Useful Contacts

Tourist Offices

Office Tourisme Saumurois, 16 r Hotels 49260 PUY NOTRE DAME (LE)
Tel: 0033 (0)2 41 38 87 30   www.ot-saumur.fr   infos@ot-saumur.fr

Office de Tourisme du Pays Thouarsais, 3 Bis bd Pierre Curie 79100 THOUARS
Tel: 0033 (0)5 49 66 17 65   www.tourisme-pays-thouarsais.fr
accueil@tourisme-pays-thouarsais

Cyber Cafe

Le Café des Arts, 53 r St Médard 79100 THOUARS Tel: 0033 (0)5 49 66 09 13
Dream's Café, 38 av Henri Barbusse 79100 THOUARS Tel: 0033 (0)5 49 66 11 71
Café de la Passerelle, 7 av Emile Zola 79100 THOUARS Tel: 0033 (0)5 49 96 11 97

Doctor

Body Sylviane, 1 r Lamartine 79100 THOUARS Tel: 0033 (0)5 49 96 30 25

Veterinary

Colasson Christian, 22 Bis av Victor Hugo 79100 THOUARS
Tel: 0033 (0)5 49 66 70 29

Farrier

Renard Daniel, 10 r Thouet 79100 SAINT JACQUES DE THOUARS
Tel: 0033 (0)5 49 68 05 95

Thouars to Airvault 29km

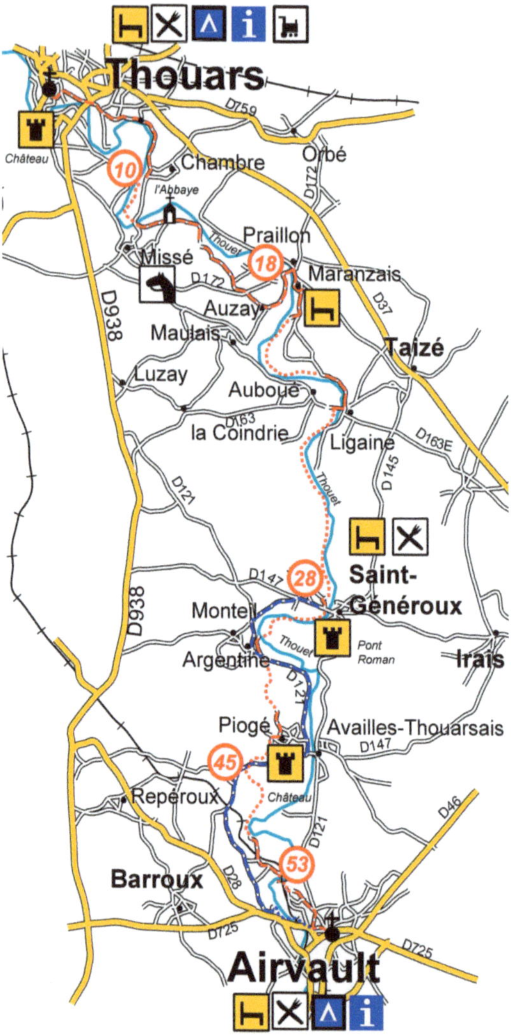

Route Summary: The section follows the meandering course of le Thouet and while generally easy going for all groups there are some river crossings beyond Saint-Généroux that could be a challenge for horse and bike riders. The alternate route follows the Thouars to Airvault cycle route signs.

Airvault is located on the River Thouet and the inhabitants are known as the Airvaudais and the Airvaudaises. A Romanesque bridge over the Thouet leads into the town. The Saint Pierre church in the centre of town was built circa 975 AD by Aldéarde, the wife of viscount Herbert I of Thouars. Rebuilt in the 11th and 12th centuries, the church was used as a stop for pilgrims on their way to Santiago de Compostela. An underground fountain is located under the square in front of the church.

Way Point	Distance	Directions	Verification Point	Compass
1		With the church of Saint Médard to the right proceed along Place Saint-Médard and rue du Grenier a Sel	GR sign	NE
2	400	Continue straight ahead on rue Félix Gelusseau	Beside *le Tour du Prince des* Galles	NE
3	90	At the crossroads continue straight ahead on rue de la Mare aux Canards		E
4	60	Bear right on the same road	GR 36 sign	SE
5	1100	At the junction bear right on rue du Moulin de Fertevault	GR 36 sign	SE
6	120	Continue straight ahead direction Fertevault	GR 36 sign	SE
7	200	Continue straight ahead down the hill	GR sign	E
8	500	Turn right on chemin de Bateloup	GR 36 sign	S
9	1300	In the village of Chambre turn right on rue du Thouet		SW
10	300	Bear right onto a grass track near house no. 31		S
11	1200	At T-junction with a minor road turn right to cross the river le Thouet		SE
12	160	At the top of a small rise continue on rue de l'Abbaye		E
13	600	At T-junction beside the war memorial turn left down the hill	Towards the'Abbaye	SE
14	1100	Bear left up the hill remaining on the road		SE
15	1500	At a T-junction with a minor road turn left		E
16	130	Bear right direction Auzay on the C4	GR sign	SE
17	600	At a crossroads in the village of Auzay turn left rue des Marronniers		N

Thouars to Airvault 29km

Way Point	Distance	Directions	Verification Point	Compass
18	900	At the T-junction turn right and cross the river towards Praillon and Maranzais		NE
19	200	Turn right into Maranzais on rue du Thouet	Aire de Pic-nique	S
20	200	Take the right fork onto rue de la Chapelle	GR sign	SE
21	200	At the crossroads in Maranzais turn right onto rue de Bourdet		S
22	500	At fork, bear right beside house no. 20	Keeping parallel to the river on the right	S
23	2300	Continue straight ahead with the river on the right		SE
24	1000	At the crossroads in Ligaine turn right and cross the bridge	GR sign	W
25	400	Turn sharp left down the hill	Just before the sign for Auboué	S
26	2200	Continue straight ahead with the river on the left		S
27	2000	On entering the village take the left fork		S
28	180	At the T-junction in front of the blue gates turn left and go down the hill. **Note:-** the track ahead includes a number of river crossings using narrow wooden bridges and other obstacles. An alternative for horse and bike riders is to turn right and then the first left to follow the excellent cycle route to Airvault marked by the small concrete signs. The main route is finally rejoined at Way Point #59 on the entry to Airvault centre	GR sign	SE

Thouars to Airvault 29km

Way Point	Distance	Directions	Verification Point	Compass
29	90	Turn right down an unmade track just before reaching the bridge	Roman bridge ahead	W
30	700	Turn left over a small wooden bridge and turn right keeping the river on the right	GR sign	SW
31	600	At T-junction turn right towards the river		W
32	190	Turn left beside the river and then right to take the bridge over the river before turning left on rue du Gué de Preliou		S
33	180	Turn left to go directly beside the river, rue des Hallieres	House no. 2 on the right	S
34	170	At the T-junction in Argentine turn left on rue de la Maison Forte		SE
35	100	Just before the Argentine exit sign turn right up a steep grass track	GR sign	S
36	1200	Continue straight ahead in the direction of the village of Piogé		S
37	500	At junction bear right into the village on rue de la Touche		S
38	130	At the T-junction turn right into the village		W
39	100	Take the left fork on rue du Château		SW
40	100	Fork left and left again direction Château	Beside stone pillar, GR sign	S
41	40	Facing the château entrance turn sharp right down the hill on a grass track into the woods	GR sign	SW
42	90	Fork right on the track down the hill		S
43	180	At the crossroads in the track, just after crossing the river, turn right		SW

Thouars to Airvault 29km

Way Point	Distance	Directions	Verification Point	Compass
44	400	At junction with a minor road turn right up the hill		SW
45	200	Turn left off the road onto a gravel track	GR sign	SE
46	300	Take the right fork towards the trees		SE
47	300	Fork right onto the grass track towards the pylon on the sky-line		S
48	90	Keep left	GR sign	S
49	200	At junction in the track bear right		SW
50	300	Continue straight ahead into the trees		S
51	1000	Continue straight ahead on the road	GR sign	SE
52	300	Take the left fork direction Salin	GR sign	SE
53	170	Before the level crossing turn right onto a grass track	GR sign	SE
54	60	Bear right keeping the railway track on your left	GR sign	S
55	300	At the top of a small rise beside an electricity transformer bear left into a grassy area	GR sign	SE
56	80	Fork right onto the tarmac – rue de Courte Vallée		SE
57	300	Continue straight ahead up the hill	Camp-site to the right	SE
58	400	At the mini-roundabout take the first exit – route d'Availles		S
59	300	At the mini-roundabout turn left – rue du Moulin Noir	GR sign	E
60	100	Continue straight ahead ignoring the GR sign to the right (unnecessary diversion)		E

Thouars to Airvault 29km

Way Point	Distance	Directions	Verification Point	Compass
61	200	At the mini-roundabout turn right and right again on route Saint-Jérôme		SE
62	70	Cointinue straight ahead on route Saint-Jérôme to avoid steep flight of steps.		SE
63	120	Arrive in Airvault centre beside l'église Saint-Pierre d'Airvault	GR sign	

Accommodation Hotel/ B&B	Price	Opening	Animals
La Closeraie du Val de Thouet, 24 r Thouet Maranzais 79100 TAIZE Tel: 0033 (0)5 49 68 02 76	B2	All Year	
[78m] AU BON ACCUEIL, 2 R Eglise 79600 SAINT GÉNÉROUX Tel: 0033 (0)5 49 67 55 35	B2	All Year	
Les Trois Marie, 1 Bis r Chaperonnière 79600 AIRVAULT Tel: 0033 (0)5 49 94 63 90	B2	All Year	
Hôtel du Cygne, 10 r Gare 79600 AIRVAULT Tel: 0033 (0)5 49 64 70 61	B2	All Year	
M. vilain, Le Vieux Chateau, 6 rue Brelucan 79600 AIRVAULT Tel: 0033 (0)5 49 64 25 78 levieuxchateau@free.fr	B2	All Year	
M. et Mme Simmoneau, 5 Imp. Jariette-Barroux 79600 AIRVAULT Tel: 0033 (0)5 49 64 70 65	B2	All Year	

Camping	Price	Opening	Animals
Camping de Courte Vallée, 8 r Courte Vallée 79600 AIRVAULT Tel: 0033 (0)5 49 64 70 65	B1	All Year	

Camping Municipal du Pont Vernay 79600 AIRVAULT Tel: 0033 (0)5 49 64 70 13 mairie-airvault@cc-parthenay.fr

Equestrian Centre

Les Ecuries du Chatelier, Le Chatelier 79100 MISSE Tel: 0033 (0)5 49 96 60 47

Thouars to Airvault 29km

Useful Contacts
Tourist Offices
Office de Tourisme, 2 rue de l'église 79600 SAINT-GENEROUX
Tel: 0033 (0)5 49 70 84 03

Communauté de Communes de l'Airvaudais, 33 Place des Promenades, 79600 AIRVAULT
Tel: 05 49 64 93 48 office-tourisme-airvaudais@wanadoo.fr

Doctor
Merle Michel, 23 Bis r Poste 79600 AIRVAULT   Tel: 0033 (0)5 49 64 48 24

Veterinary
Vouillon Laurent Serre Pierre, 17 pl Promenades 79600 AIRVAULT
Tel: 0033 (0)5 49 64 70 74

Farrier
Barbier Arnaud, 8 r Marronniers Maisoncelle 79600 ASSAIS LES JUMEAUX
Tel: 0033 (0)5 49 70 05 59

Thouars to Airvault 29km

Accommodation Hotel / B&B	Price	Opening	Animals
PR Roseline Marcaillou, 15 Grand'rue théophane Vénard 79600 ST LOUP SUR THOUET Tel: 0033 (0)5 49 70 25 63 roseline.mercaillou@club-internet.fr	B2	All Year	🐴
Le Relais du Chapeau Rouge, 33 rue Théophane Vénard 79600 Saint Loup Lamairé Tél. 05.49.64.68.08 lechapeaurouge@laposte.net www.lerelaisduchapeaurouge.fr	B2	All Year	🐴
Hotel Bar La Meilleraye, 93 bd Meilleraye 79200 PARTHENAY Tel:0033 (0)5 49 95 20 26	B2	All Year	🐴
Hôtel Restaurant du Nord, 86 av Gén de Gaulle 79200 PARTHENAY Tel: 0033 (0)5 49 94 29 11	B2	All Year	🐴
Les Jardins Saint-Laurent, 15 r Carnot 79200 PARTHENAY Tel: 0033 (0)5 49 71 28 30 jardins.st.laurent@orange.fr	B2	All Year	🐴
Hôtel Saint-Jacques, 13 av 114ème RI 79200 PARTHENAY Tel: 0033 (0)5 49 64 33 33	B2	All Year	🐴
Hôtel Bar Le Castille, 6 av 114ème RI 79200 PARTHENAY Tel: 0033 (0)5 49 64 13 67 lecastille@cc-parthenay.fr	B3	All Year	🐴
Le Commerce, 30 bd Edgar Quinet 79200 PARTHENAY Tel: 0033 (0)5 49 94 36 13	B2	All Year	🐴
Au Relais des Lilas, 197 av Aristide Briand 79200 PARTHENAY Tel: 0033 (0)5 49 94 06 44	B2	All Year	🐴
Pied Yvan, 7 r Bélisaire Ledain 79200 PARTHENAY Tel: 0033 (0)5 49 70 22 00	B2	All Year	🐴
PR Hôtel Bar Le Castille, 6 av 114ème RI 79200 PARTHENAY Tel: 0033 (0)5 49 64 13 67 lecastille@cc-parthenay.fr	B2	All Year	🐴
Caillaud Annie, 51 rue Louis Aguillon 79200 Parthenay Tel: 0033 (0)549941269 annie.caillaud@wanadoo.fr	B2	All Year	🐴
Equestrian Centre			

Ecurie de Puymoreau, 3 Rte Tourneur d'Aumont Ld Puymoreau 17400 BENÂTE (LA)
Mobile: 0033 (0)6 13 27 96 45 **Note:** 4.5km from St Loup sur Thouet

Parc Equestre de Parthenay, 11 r Brossard 79200 PARTHENAY
Mobile: 0033 (0)6 80 42 10 12

Airvault to Parthenay 30.9km

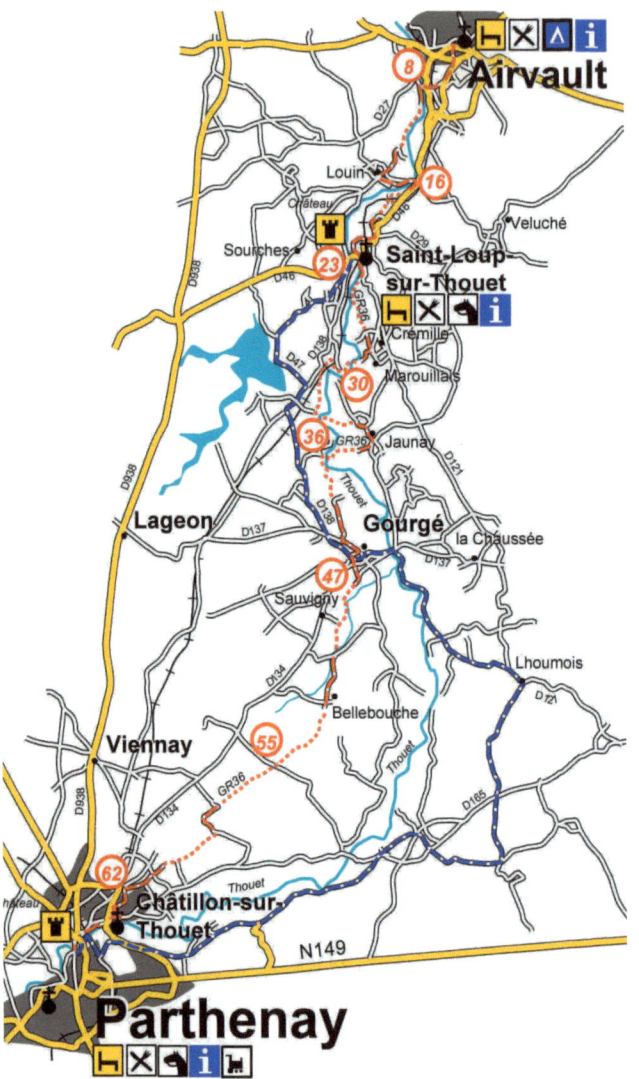

Route Summary: this is a long section continuing to follow the course of le Thouet. The primary route follows quiet country lanes but involves a number of river crossings via stepping stones or fords prior to Gourgé, while there are also tricky obstacles for horse and bike riders on the main route's entry into Châtillon-sur-Thouet and Parthenay. The alternate route again follows the Vallée de Thouet cycle route from Saint-Loup-sur-Thouet via Gourgé to Parthenay. The alternate route adds 6.3 kilometres to the overall section length, however, walkers pressed for time could reduce the section by 2.1 kilometres by taking the alternate route from Saint-Loup-sur-Thouet to Gourgé.

Way Point	Distance	Directions	Verification Point	Compass
1		Facing the church entrance, turn right and proceed on rue de la Poste with the covered market, les Halles, on your right. **Note:**- the GR signs follow a tortuous route through the streets of Airvault we suggest this more direct exit		S
2	40	Cross rue des Halles and continue on rue de la Poste		S
3	30	Bear right on *rue de la* Ferronnerie		S
4	150	Continue straight ahead rue Constant Balquet		S
5	200	Bear right on the D43, rue des Sablières	GR sign	SW
6	300	Turn right onto rue de la Croix Barbouine		SW
7	300	Bear right towards Pont de Vernay		W
8	80	At the crossroads go straight ahead over the bridge and immediately turn left	Parthenay cycle route sign	SW
9	1800	Take the left fork remaining on the cycle route	Beside stone crucifix – Croix Barrault	SW
10	500	At the crossroads go straight ahead on rue du Four Banal		SW
11	300	With the church on the left turn left down the hill	Village of Louin	SW
12	60	Turn left down rue de Genêts	Beside café l'Union	E
13	160	Continue straight ahead on rue de Genêts. **Note:**- ignore GR sign as the route returns to the main road in a few metres		E
14	180	Continue straight ahead on rue de Genêts		E
15	600	At the roundabout take the first exit across the bridge and then turn right on the D46		S
16	130	Just before the sign for le Fief Barreau bear right on a dirt track		SW

Airvault to Parthenay 30.9km

Way Point	Distance	Directions	Verification Point	Compass
17	500	At a crossroads in the track turn left under the railway bridge and then right		SW
18	600	Continue straight ahead with houses on the left		S
19	400	Turn right on the D46 to enter Saint-Loup-sur-Thouet		S
20	80	Turn right down a "No Entry" road, Grand rue de Brard		SW
21	200	Turn right over the level-crossing		W
22	300	Turn left into the narrow street of part timbered houses, towards the church	Château to the right	S
23	300	At the T-junction turn left on the D46 in the direction of Airvault. **Note:-** to avoid the stepping stone and ford river crossings go straight ahead and take the D138 in the direction of Gourgé and follow the cycle route signs for Gourgé and then Parthenay. The alternate route to Gourgé is 2.1km shorter than the main route		SE
24	140	Bear right on the D121		SE
25	60	Bear right onto a gravel track with the river directly on the right	GR sign	S
26	1600	At the top of the rise turn left	Line of trees on the left	SE
27	200	Turn right onto the minor road and then immediately left		S
28	400	At the crossroads turn right down the hill	GR sign	SW
29	200	Turn right down the hill	Beside house no. 8	SW
30	300	Continue straight across the river		SW
31	130	At top of the hill bear left on the tarmac	GR sign	SW
32	200	Bear left and then immediately right	GR sign	W

Airvault to Parthenay 30.9km

Way Point	Distance	Directions	Verification Point	Compass
33	600	At the T-junction at the top of the hill turn left down the hill		S
34	800	At the T-junction in front of the farm – Rochemanue – turn left	Pond on the right	SE
35	70	Bear right on an unmade track	Keep house no. 4 to the left	SE
36	120	Cross the river. **Note:-** horses would need to wade and cyclists carry their bikes		E
37	900	At junction with a minor road turn right and remain on the road. **Note:-** the GR sign leads to an unnecessary dog-leg returning to the road at the next Way Point		SE
38	200	At the T-junction turn right towards Jaunay	GR sign	S
39	400	Turn right direction le Champ Pineau	GR sign	W
40	700	Continue straight ahead onto the unmade track	GR sign	SW
41	400	Cross the river. **Note:-** the water here is probably too deep for most horses to safely ford the river		NW
42	200	On reaching the tarmac at the top of the hill turn sharp left	GR sign	S
43	1200	At T-junction turn right towards the village of Gourgé	GR sign	S
44	900	At the crossroads turn left direction Moulin Neuf	Crucifix ahead	SE
45	400	At crossroads turn right on rue du Teil	GR sign	SW
46	200	At the T-junction turn left towards la Poste		SE

Airvault to Parthenay 30.9km

Airvault to Parthenay 30.9km

Way Point	Distance	Directions	Verification Point	Compass
47	150	Turn right on rue de la Commanderie. **Note:**- the alternate route crosses the main route here. To follow the alternate route and avoid the obstacles on entry to Châtillon and Parthenay continue straight ahead following the cycle route signs to Parthenay. The alternate route adds 8.4km to the length of the remainder of the section.	GR sign	SW
48	120	Turn left on rue de l'Archère	GR sign	S
49	300	Turn right towards le Chemin, keeping house on the right	GR sign	SW
50	300	Take the left fork	GR sign	S
51	900	Continue straight ahead	Large farm on the right	S
52	700	At junction with a road turn right and then bear left, direction Belle Bouche		S
53	1200	Take the left fork		S
54	1000	Take the right fork	GR sign	SW
55	1000	At crossroads, cross straight over onto the gravel track towards le Petit Fontenioux	GR sign	SW
56	2200	At a crossroads in the track turn left	GR sign	SE
57	400	Turn right between trees	Wooden gate on the left	SW
58	1100	Continue straight ahead with a farm on the right, la Jousselinière	GR sign	SW
59	600	At crossroads with a more major road, go straight ahead on the minor road	GR sign	SW
60	300	Continue straight ahead into Châtillon-sur-Thouet		SW
61	400	At a roundabout bear left on the main road		SW
62	130	At the second roundabout turn left on avenue de l'Hermitage		SW
63	400	Fork right down the hill on avenue de l'Ebaupin	GR sign	NW
64	130	Just before the roundabout turn left down a gravel track	GR sign	S

Way Point	Distance	Directions	Verification Point	Compass
65	40	Turn sharp right to go down the gravel track in the park		W
66	50	Continue straight ahead up the hill	GR sign	S
67	110	Turn sharp left on the tarmac	GR sign	E
68	50	Turn right with water on the right		S
69	120	Take the left fork up the hill		S
70	50	Bear left and then immediately right up a steep track between low walls	GR sign	NE
71	40	Bear right up a flight of steps and then bear left with the church on the right		E
72	60	With the church on the right bear right down the hill on avenue de l'Ebaupin		SE
73	60	Bear right and then left on côte du Rouget Barbet	GR sign	SW
74	300	Turn right to go under the road bridge	River on the left	W
75	70	Continue straight ahead beside the river		W
76	150	At the top of the steps turn left with the river on the left		W
77	180	Cross the grassed area to the left of the telegraph pole close to the river	GR sign	SW
78	400	At the top of the rise cross over the main road onto chemin du Rosaire	GR sign	SW
79	130	Turn left on rue du Calvaire and then left again on Grande rue de Four	GR sign	S
80	90	Turn right on rue *du Faub*ourg Saint-Jacques		S
81	150	Arrive in Parthenay at the Porte Saint-Jacques		

Airvault to Parthenay 30.9km

Airvault to Parthenay 30.9km

Accommodation Hotel/ B&B	Price	Opening	Animals
PR Roseline Mercaillou, 15 Grand'rue théophane Vénard 79600 ST LOUP SUR THOUET Tel: 0033 (0)5 49 70 25 63 roseline.mercaillou@club-internet.fr	B2	All Year	🐴
Le Relais du Chapeau Rouge, 33 rue Théophane Vénard 79600 Saint Loup Lamairé Tél. 05.49.64.68.08 lechapeaurouge@laposte.net www.lerelaisduchapeaurouge.fr	B2	All Year	🐴
Hotel Bar La Meilleraye, 93 bd Meilleraye 79200 PARTHENAY Tel:0033 (0)5 49 95 20 26	B2	All Year	🐴
Hôtel Restaurant du Nord, 86 av Gén de Gaulle 79200 PARTHENAY Tel: 0033 (0)5 49 94 29 11	B2	All Year	🐴
Les Jardins Saint-Laurent, 15 r Carnot 79200 PARTHENAY Tel: 0033 (0)5 49 71 28 30 jardins.st.laurent@orange.fr	B2	All Year	🐴
Hôtel Saint-Jacques, 13 av 114ème RI 79200 PARTHENAY Tel: 0033 (0)5 49 64 33 33	B2	All Year	🐴
Le Commerce, 30 bd Edgar Quinet 79200 PARTHENAY Tel: 0033 (0)5 49 94 36 13	B2	All Year	🐴
Au Relais des Lilas, 197 av Aristide Briand 79200 PARTHENAY Tel: 0033 (0)5 49 94 06 44	B2	All Year	🐴
Pied Yvan, 7 r Bélisaire Ledain 79200 PARTHENAY Tel: 0033 (0)5 49 70 22 00	B2	All Year	🐴
PR Hôtel Bar Le Castille, 6 av 114ème RI 79200 PARTHENAY Tel: 0033 (0)5 49 64 13 67 lecastille@cc-parthenay.fr	B2	All Year	🐴
Caillaud Annie, 51 rue Louis Aguillon 79200 Parthenay Tel: 0033 (0)549941269 annie.caillaud@wanadoo.fr	B2	All Year	🐴

Equestrian Centre

Ecurie de Puymoreau, 3 Rte Tourneur d'Aumont Ld Puymoreau 17400 BENÂTE (LA) Mobile: 0033 (0)6 13 27 96 45 **Note:** 4.5km from St Loup sur Thouet

Parc Equestre de Parthenay, 11 r Brossard 79200 PARTHENAY Mobile: 0033 (0)6 80 42 10 12

Camping	Price	Opening	Animals
Camping le Bois Vert, rte de Boisseau 79200 PARTHENAY Tel: 0033 (0)5 49 64 78 43 roseline.mercaillou@club-internet.fr	B2	All Year	

Useful Contacts

Tourist Offices
Office de Tourisme, 8 r Vaux St Jacques 79200 PARTHENAY
Tel: 0033 (0)5 49 64 24 24   http://portail.cc-parthenay.fr/Portail2007
office-tourisme@cc-parthenay.fr

Doctor
Ranaivo Robert, 52 av Gén de Gaulle 79200 PARTHENAY
Tel: 0033 (0)9 71 53 76 53

Veterinary
Cabinet Vétérinaire De Groof, 6 bd Ambroise Paré 79200 PARTHENAY
Tel: 0033 (0)5 49 64 33 64

Farrier
Cohendet Eric, 2 r Violettes 79200 CHATILLON SUR THOUET
Mobile: 0033 (0)6 07 11 04 62

Legend has it that **Parthenay** was created with a wave of the fairy Melusine's wand. However the name of Parthenay first appears in written records at the beginning of the 11th century and there is no evidence of previous significant human occupation in the Middle Ages. The castle, situated on an easily defended site at the tip of the rocky promontory surrounded by the loop of the river, was built in the 13th century. At the same time the outer fortifications protecting the citadel, and the town itself, were completed. Parthenay benefited from being on one of the branches of the St. James Way to Santiago de Compostela. The main fortified gate, by which pilgrims would enter the town, still bears the name of Saint James. Through the gateway, on rue de la Citadelle, the attractively simple Romanesque church of Ste-Croix faces the mairie across a small garden, which offers views over the ramparts and the gully of St-Jacques, with its medieval houses and vegetable plots climbing

the opposite slope. Further along rue de la Citadelle is a house where Cardinal Richelieu used to visit his grandfather, and then a handsome but badly damaged Romanesque door, all that remains of the castle chapel of Notre-Dame-de-la-Couldre. Practically nothing is left of the castle itself, but from the tip of the spur where it once stood you can look down on the twin-towered gateway and the Pont St-Jacques, a thirteenth-century bridge through which the nightly flocks of pilgrims poured into the town for shelter and security. To reach it, turn left under the Tour de l'Horloge and down the medieval lane known as Vaux St-Jacques. The lane is highly evocative of that period, with crooked half-timbered dwellings crowding up to the bridge.

Parthenay to Champdeniers-Saint-Denis 28km

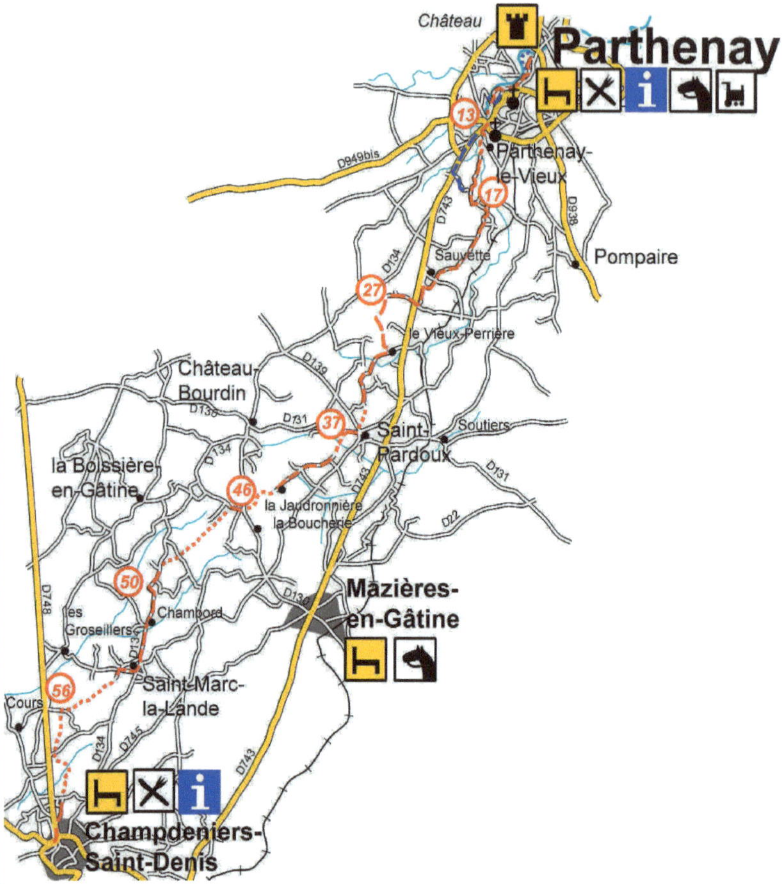

Route Summary: after the exit from Parthenay, with horse-riders negotiating the alternate route to avoid the unguarded and narrow bridge, the route progresses easily along minor roads and tracks. On a number of occasions we have chosen to remain on the road to avoid dog-legs which add unnecessary distance to the route. If you wish to avoid the road the GR signs will direct you around the dog-leg tracks. Champdeniers has limited accommodation as do the other small villages between Parthenay and Niort. It is advisable to telephone ahead to secure accommodation particularly in the high season. The tourist office in Parthenay can help.

Way Point	Distance	Directions	Verification Point	Compass
1		From the Porte Saint Jacques continue in the direction of the centre of Parthenay on rue de la vau Saint-Jacques	Pass tourist Office on the right	S
2	200	Take the second right in the direction of l'Eglise Notre Dame de la Couldre on rue Parmentier	GR sign	NW
3	120	Turn left up the steps on chemin de la Citadelle. **Note**:- horse and bike riders should continue to the road junction, bike riders should then bear right and left progressing between the city walls and château (on your left) and the river (on your right) to the foot of the steps at Way Point #6	GR sign	SW
4	250	At the top of the steps turn left and continue on rue de la Citadelle		S
5	300	Pass through Porte de la Citadelle and turn immediately right to descend the steep flight of steps. **Note**:- horse riders should continue straight ahead onto the rue Jean-Jaures before turning right and descending on Côte Saint-Paul towards the river bridge and rejoining the main route at Way Point #7	GR sign	SW
6	130	At the foot of the steps turn left beside the city walls	GR sign	SW
7	70	Turn left onto rue Jean Mermoz	GR sign	SW
8	200	Fork right off the main road onto rue du Pied de Bouc	GR sign	W
9	300	Continue straight ahead onto a gravel path	GR sign	SW
10	500	Continue straight ahead keeping the foot-bridge to your right		S
11	400	Turn left with second foot bridge to your right	GR sign	E
12	150	At the end of the gravel track turn right keeping the car park on your left and towards the GR sign on the tree. Then proceed on the busy boulevard Georges Clemenceau towards the roundabout	Leisure Centre to the left	SW

Parthenay to Champdeniers-Saint-Denis 28km

Parthenay to Champdenier-Saint-Denis 28km

Way Point	Distance	Directions	Verification Point	Compass
13	300	Go straight ahead at the roundabout and then turn almost immediately left on rue de l'Eglise – direction Eglise de Parthenay le Vieux. **Note:-** there is a narrow bridge ahead which will not be possible for horses although in good conditions it may be possible for confident horses to ford the river. The alternative route is to follow the main road taking the first left after the next roundabout towards the farm le Bois des Grais and rejoining the main route at Way Point #17	GR sign	S
14	200	Pass the church on your left and then turn right on route de Coteau	GR sign	S
15	120	Turn right off the road onto a grass track direction la Fontaine de Rézard	GR sign	S
16	400	Take the bridge over the river. **Note:-** the bridge is not safe for horses		S
17	1100	At junction with a minor road turn left	GR sign	SE
18	700	Turn right onto a gravel track	GR sign	S
19	400	Continue straight ahead on the unmade track		SW
20	1000	Continue straight ahead		SW
21	800	At the junction with a minor road cross straight over towards the hamlet of Sauvette		SW
22	200	Continue straight ahead		NW
23	130	Bear left with farm buildings on the right		W
24	90	At a T-junction just before the main road turn left and proceed parallel to the main road on your right		S
25	500	Cross over the main road and turn right direction la Bezochère		NW
26	500	Continue straight ahead		W
27	200	Turn left off the road onto a grassy track	Sign for chemin privée to the right	SW

Way Point	Distance	Directions	Verification Point	Compass
28	500	Continue straight ahead direction Saint-Pardoux	GR sign	SW
29	120	Turn left down a narrow track	GR sign	SE
30	200	Continue straight ahead		S
31	600	Track emerges on a minor road turn right up the hill	Beside le Vieux Perrière	SW
32	400	Continue straight ahead	Pass turning to la Baubière on the right, GR sign	SW
33	400	At a T-junction turn left	GR sign	S
34	700	Turn left off the road onto a grass track	GR sign	S
35	800	At the T-junction in Saint-Pardoux turn left towards the church	GR sign	S
36	150	Turn right on the D131 direction Château-Bourdin		W
37	300	Turn left onto an unmade track beside house No. 19	GR sign	SW
38	400	Take the left fork on the track	GR sign	SW
39	200	Continue straight ahead beside la Mimardière	GR sign	SW
40	200	At T-junction with a minor road turn right	GR sign	W
41	500	Remain on the main road. **Note:-** the GR leaves to the right to take an unnecessary dog leg that returns to the road at Way Point #45		SW
42	200	Continue straight ahead direction la Jaudronnière		SW
43	700	Continue straight ahead beside la Jaudronnière	Derelict house to the right	SW
44	140	Continue straight ahead on the gravel track		W
45	200	Bear left with the Croix de l'Hemais on the left	GR rejoins from the right	SW
46	600	At the junction with the D130 cross over and bear right in the direction of le Bois Pillon	GR sign	W
47	400	Turn left onto a gravel track following the GR36 towards Niort	GR sign	SW

Parthenay to Champdenier-Saint-Denis 28km

Parthenay to Champdenier-Saint-Denis 28km

Way Point	Distance	Directions	Verification Point	Compass
48	1900	Cross over the minor road and continue straight ahead on the track, the farm of la Roche Marot to the right	GR sign	SW
49	600	Track emerges onto a minor road (D134) turn left	GR sign	SW
50	500	Remain on road. **Note:**- the GR leaves to the right to take an unnecessary dog leg that returns to the road at Way Point #51		S
51	1100	GR36 returns from the right, continue on the road		S
52	180	Remain on road. **Note:**- the GR leaves to the left, just after the quarry, to take an unnecessary dog leg that returns to the road at Way Point #53		S
53	800	Bear right on the D134 direction Champdeniers	GR sign	SW
54	180	In Saint-Marc-la-Lande, turn right in the direction of les Groseillers	Pass church on the left	W
55	400	Just after leaving the village turn left onto a gravel track	GR sign	SW
56	2000	At a crossroads in the tracks turn left	GR sign	S
57	600	Bear right on the track	GR sign	S
58	400	At junction with a minor road turn right, passing the farm — la Vergne	GR sign	SW
59	110	Shortly after passing la Vergne turn left onto a track	GR sign	SE
60	600	Bear right between 2 lines of trees	GR sign	SW
61	200	Bear left with a line of trees on the left	GR sign	S
62	400	Continue straight ahead down the hill on rue du Stade	GR sign	S
63	200	At the mini-roundabout take the second exit remaining on rue du Stade towards the town centre	GR sign	S
64	400	At T-junction turn left with petrol station on the left	GR sign	S
65	300	Bear right direction Fontenay on the D745		SW
66	160	Arrive in Champdeniers-Saint-Denis centre at the junction between rue Pineau and rue de Genève		

Accommodation Hotel/ B&B	Price	Opening	Animals
Château du Petit Chêne, Le Petit Chêne 79310 MAZIERES EN GATINE Tel: 0033 (0)5 49 63 28 42 **Note:** 3km off the route on D130	B2	All Year	
La Grolerie, La Grolerie 79220 CHAMPDENIERS SAINT DENIS Tel: 0033 (0)5 49 25 66 11	B2	All Year	
Chambres d'Hôtes du Paradis, 5 Place du Paradis 79220 CHAMPDENIERS-SAINT-DENIS Tel: 0033 (0)5 49 25 87 22	B2	All Year	

Equestrian Centre

Centre Equestre de la Galipote, Le Beugnon 79310 MAZIERES EN GATINE Tel: 0033 (0)5 49 63 12 72 **Note:** 3km off the route on D130

Useful Contacts

Tourist Offices

Syndicat D'Initiative, 7 pl St Antoine 79220 CHAMPDENIERS SAINT DENIS Tel: 0033 (0)5 49 25 86 54

Doctor

Aupy Jean Marc, 15 pl Champ de Foire 79220 CHAMPDENIERS SAINT DENIS Tel: 0033 (0)5 49 25 65 58

Veterinary

Cabinet Vétérinaire, pl St Antoine 79220 CHAMPDENIERS SAINT DENIS Tel: 0033 (0)5 49 25 80 45

Farrier

Rongieras Philippe, L'Etang 79220 COURS Tel: 0033 (0)5 49 04 20 27 Mobile: 0033 (0)9 63 49 94 47

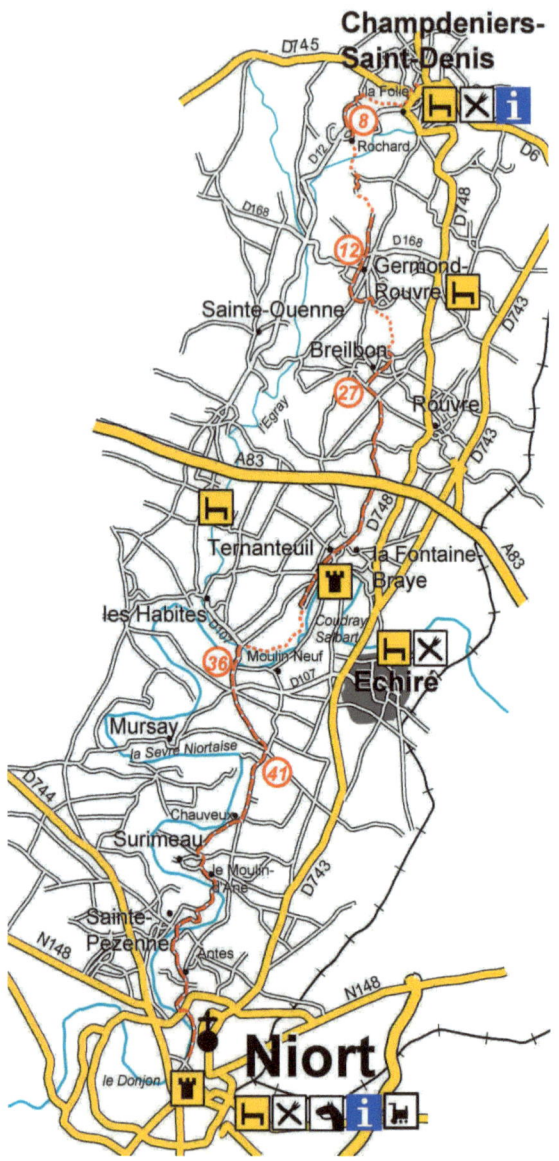

Champdeniers-Saint-Denis to Niort 24.8km

Route Summary: This section is undertaken largely on quiet country roads interspersed with broad farm tracks. In general the going is easy for all groups with a few short but steep climbs. On a number of occasions we have again chosen to deviate from the GR36 by remaining on the quiet country roads where we feel the GR36 adds distance or complexity, but no advantage. The entry to Niort successfully bypasses the heaviest traffic following minor roads by the river-side.

Way Point	Distance	Directions	Verification Point	Compass
1		From the junction of rue Pineau and rue de Genève take rue Pineau	GR sign	NW
2	200	Turn left onto a gravel track between birch trees	GR sign	S
3	400	At the metal barriers turn right on the D12 and then immediately right again onto a dirt track. **Note**:- at time of writing the barriers could be opened. If locked then it would be necessary to retrace the route to Way Point #1 and take rue de Genève and then turn right on the D12 – rue de Folie to return to this point	GR sign	W
4	500	Bear right remaining on the same track		NW
5	400	At junction with a minor road turn left towards the farm of le Bouchet		SW
6	400	Bear left on the track keeping the quarry to your right		S
7	400	At the T-junction with the D12 turn left	GR sign	E
8	130	Turn right off the main road and down the hill direction les Rochards	GR sign	S
9	800	At the top of the steep hill continue straight ahead	GR sign	S
10	70	In front of a small-holding – les Retraisses – bear left in the direction of Niort	GR sign	E
11	120	Turn right off the road down an unmade track	GR sign	S
12	1700	Emerge onto a road and continue straight ahead on chemin du Bourneau, keeping the cemetery to the left	GR sign	SW
13	150	Remain on chemin du Bourneau, taking the left-most of 3 turnings keeping white houses to your right	GR sign	SW
14	200	At the crossroads, in Germon-Rouvre, continue straight ahead on chemin de Midard	GR sign	SW
15	400	Take the left fork	GR sign	SE

Champdeniers-Saint-Denis to Niort 24.8km

Way Point	Distance	Directions	Verification Point	Compass
16	180	Cross straight over the minor road to continue on the track	GR sign	E
17	200	At the junction with the main road turn left and then immediately right down the hill	GR sign	SE
18	300	Continue straight ahead on a grass track, les Moussandières to the left	GR sign	SE
19	800	Take the right fork down the hill		SW
20	200	At a T-junction in the tracks turn left	GR sign	SE
21	100	Keep left	GR sign	SE
22	120	At the junction with the road turn right towards the village of Beilbon	GR sign	SW
23	50	Cross straight over the road to continue on the track	GR sign	SW
24	300	Track emerges onto a road turn left on chemin de Minée	GR sign	SW
25	60	Bear left on chemin de Minée	GR sign	SW
26	120	Continue straight ahead to leave the village	GR sign	SW
27	200	At a T-junction turn left	GR sign	SE
28	300	Cross straight over the minor road to continue on the track	GR sign	S
29	800	At a crossroads in the tracks continue straight ahead	GR sign	S
30	2100	Keep straight ahead. **Note:-** the GR36 turns to the left at this point, but at the time of writing various construction activities blocked the path ahead. The route will rejoin the GR after crossing the river Sèvre Niortaise at Way Point #38		SW
31	200	Continue straight ahead on Grande rue de Ternanteuil		SW
32	50	Keep right through the village of Ternanteuil		SW

Champdeniers-Saint-Denis to Niort 24.8km

Way Point	Distance	Directions	Verification Point	Compass
33	200	Continue straight ahead onto rue de la Fuie	Ruins of Coudray-Salbart visible high on the far side of the river	SW
34	500	Take the left fork down the hill		SW
35	200	Continue straight ahead down the hill		S
36	500	With the farmhouse on your left turn right onto a gravel track	Parallel to the river	SW
37	1800	The track emerges on the D107 turn left and cross over the river bridge		S
38	400	Continue straight ahead up the hill with the farm of Gué Moreau to the right	GR sign	S
39	400	At the crossroads continue straight ahead. **Note:-** the route turns away from the GR to save an unnecessary distance of 1.5km		SE
40	1300	At the complex junction take the second turning on the right direction Niort	Crucifix to your left	SW
41	200	Continue straight ahead. The GR36 rejoins from the right		S
42	1300	Turn right onto chemin de Chauveux	GR sign	SW
43	1000	At the road junction turn left on rue de la Berlandière	GR sign	E
44	160	Turn right onto chemin de la Berlandière	GR sign	S
45	200	At the T-junction turn left up the hill	GR sign	SE
46	200	Turn right onto rue du Moulin d'Ane	GR sign	SW
47	1000	Turn left on rue de Coquelonne	GR sign	SW
48	700	Turn left over the footbridge	GR sign	SE
49	180	Turn right onto rue de la Maison Neuve	GR sign	S
50	800	At junction bear right over a small bridge on rue d'Antes	GR sign	S
51	300	Take the right fork remaining on rue d'Antes	GR sign	S

Way Point	Distance	Directions	Verification Point	Compass
51	300	Take the right fork remaining on rue d'Antes	GR sign	S
52	100	Turn right onto chemin de la Source de Vivier	GR sign	S
53	400	Having passed under the ring road and just before a steep ramp turn right	GR sign, house no. 36 to the left	S
54	400	Continue straight ahead through the wrought iron gates		S
55	200	Continue straight ahead keeping the river to your right		S
56	400	Arrive in the centre of Niort beside the bridge at the junction of rue du Pont and Quai de Cronstadt	Donjon to the left	

Champdeniers-Saint-Denis to Niort 24.8km

Accommodation Hotel/ B&B	Price	Opening	Animals
Blanchard Didier, 40 chem Minée 79220 GERMOND ROUVRE Tel: 0033 (0)5 49 04 05 01	B2	All Year	🐴
CHEZ JOSETTE ET DIDIER BLANCHARD, 40, Chemin de la Minée 79220 GERMOND-ROUVRE Tel: 0033 (0)5 49 04 05 01	B2	All Year	🐴
Les Glycines, 111 rue du Bigne, Ternanteuil, 79410 ECHIRE Tel: 0033 (0)5 49 25 78 02 debbiekibble1@aol.com	B2	All Year	🐴
Gîte rural, Mme Terrade, Ternanteuil 79410 ECHIRÉ Tel: 0033 (0)5 49 25 71 34 jcterrade@club-internet.fr **Note:** Groups only	B2	All Year	🐴
Gîte rural, 231, route de la Fontaine Braye 79410 ECHIRÉ Tel: 0033 (0)5 49 778 779 **Note:** Groups only	B2	All Year	🐴
L'ATELIER, 26 rue Centrale 79000 NIORT Tel: 0033 (0)5 49 17 23 49 fabienneveillat@aol.com	B2	All Year	🐴
LA MAGNOLIERE, 16, Impasse de l'Abbaye, St Liguaire 79000 NIORT Tel: 0033 (0)5 49 35 36 06 a.marchadier@lamagnoliere.fr www.lamagnoliere.fr	B2	All Year	🐴
LE LAVOIR JAUNE, 31 rue Perrière 79000 NIORT Tel: 0033 (0)5 49 24 27 20 Mobile: 0033 (0)6 85 64 04 19 **Note:** Groups only	B2	All Year	🐴
VEILLET ANNICK 49, Square des Frères Montgolfier 79000 NIORT Tel: 0033 (0)6 86 83 24 54 veillan79@gmail.com	B1	All Year	🐴

Equestrian Centre

PONEY CLUB D ECHIRE, 70 RUE TAILLEE 79410 ECHIRE Tel: 0033 (0)5 49 05 09 26

Club Hippique Niortais, Les Sources 400 rte Aiffres 79000 NIORT Tel: 0033 (0)5 49 28 28 28

Champdeniers-Saint-Denis to Niort 24.8km

Château de Niort

Niort straddles the banks of the Sèvre Niortaise River and is best known for its Donjon de Niort or Château de Niort, a medieval castle consisting of two square towers, linked by a 15th century building. Construction of the castle was started by Henry II Plantagenet and completed by Richard the Lionheart. From the 18th century, the castle served as a prison. During the Hundred Years War Niort was alternately under French and English domination and finally, in the 14th century, was securely placed under the French crown, thanks to Du Guesclin. From the end of the century, the duc de Berry, brother of Charles V, began restoring the castle including improvements to the residential parts of the keep.

Windows were built or enlarged to give more light, fireplaces were installed in the grand hall which was itself split into two floors, and walls were painted or coated. After the Revolution the castle was sold to the district, who later passed it to the *Département*. The outer walls and its towers, in a poor state since the 17th century, the houses in the courtyard and the drawbridge had all disappeared. Classified as a monument historique in 1840, the castle today operates as a museum.

Notre-Dame church is the tallest building in the department of Deux-Sèvres. Its spire, which local legend says was constructed at the behest of the fairy Melusine, is 75 metres high. Built in the florid Gothic style, the church was modified and restored in the 17th, 18th and 19th centuries. Notre-Dame is best known for its stained glass window (late 15th to early 16th century), which depicts the Tree of Jesse and is the only remaining example of religious stained decorative glass artistry to be found in the department. The 11th century church of Saint-Andre is on the highest hill in Niort. Once again its primary feature is the stained glass in the side naves. Created by Van Guy de Tours (1963), these are made from splintered glass, are virtually unbreakable and have an uneven surface which produces its own natural light effects.

Notre-Dame, Niort

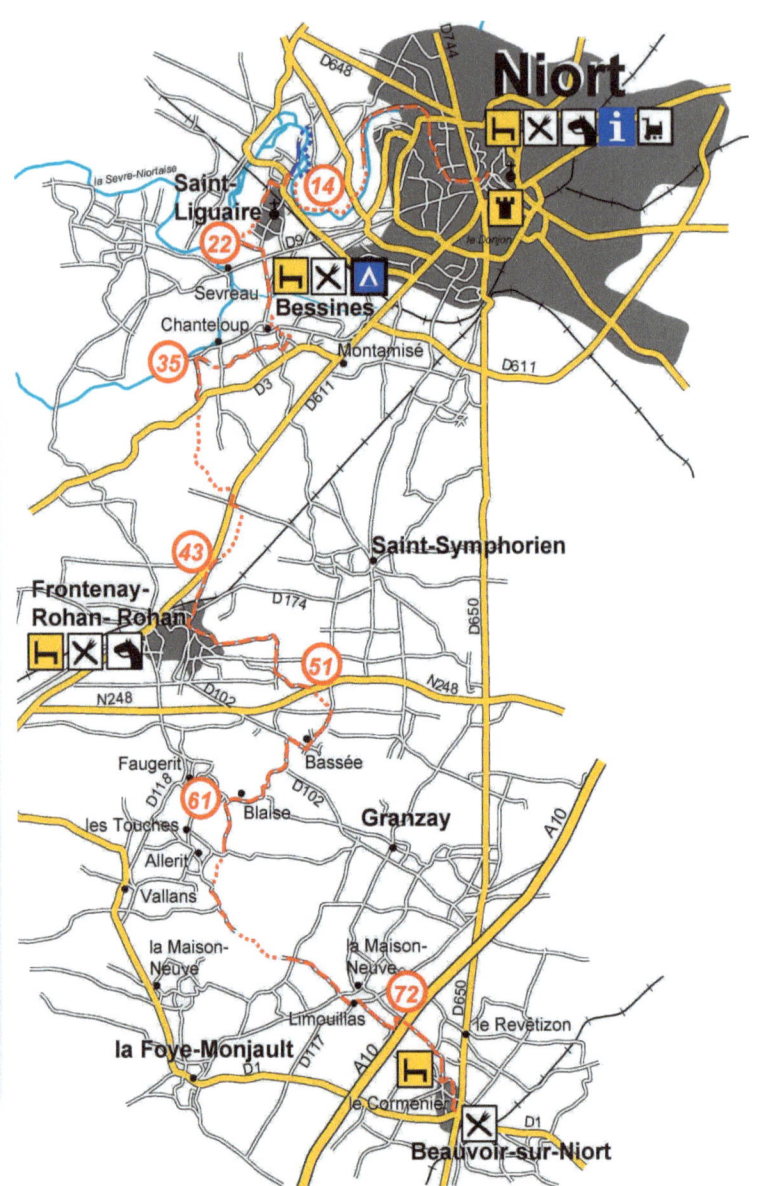

Route Summary: this is a long section that begins following the attractive but meandering course of la Sevre Niortaise and then winds its way across country on a mix of roads and tracks. Progress is hampered by the many turns in the route to avoid the busy roads in the area. There is limited accommodation at end of the section and so it is strongly advised to telephone ahead and secure a place or consider an intermediate stopping point.

Way Point	Distance	Directions	Verification Point	Compass
1		From the junction between rue du Pont and Quai de Constadt proceed over the bridge		NW
2	40	Turn left down a short flight of steps and over a bridge into the car park	GR sign	S
3	200	Emerge from the car park and turn right on quai de la Préfecture	Keep *le Donjon* on your left	SW
4	60	Turn right to cross over the river on the footbridge	GR sign	NW
5	50	After crossing the bridge turn left onto the pathway between low wooden posts	Arts centre to the right, GR sign	SW
6	90	Bear left with children's play area on the right	GR sign	W
7	60	Climb short flight of steps to the main road and turn right towards the mini-roundabout. **Note:-** the steps may prove difficult for some horses, however there is an alternate road exit from the park leading to the mini-roundabout at the next Way Point	GR sign	NW
8	80	At the mini-roundabout take the last exit on boulevard Main, direction Parking Boinot	GR sign	W
9	80	Bear left over the river onto rue de la Chamoiserie and then immediately turn right onto quai de Bell-Île, keeping the river on the right. **Note:-** the main route leads to a narrow footbridge. Horse-riders should keep straight ahead on quai Maurice Métayer with the water to the left to Way Point #11	GR sign	NW
10	1000	Turn right on the foot-ridge over the lock	GR sign	N
11	60	Turn left on quai Maurice Métayer		N
12	600	Pass under the road-bridge and continue straight ahead on quai Maurice Métayer		SW
13	2300	Bear left to progress on the path closer to the water		W

Niort to Beauvoir-sur-Niort 33.7km

Way Point	Distance	Directions	Verification Point	Compass
14	2200	Take the hand operated ferry across the river. **Note:-** the ferry will take a cycle but not horses. Horse-riders or those uncomfortable with the ferry should continue on the river-side path for approximately 1km before taking the bridge to the left and returning on rue du Moulin following the GR signs to the next Way Point		NW
15	120	Turn left and then bear right on rue du Moulin	Beside the school	W
16	100	At the T-junction turn left towards le Moulin de Saint Liguaire		S
17	110	Bear right keeping the church to your left	GR sign	S
18	120	Turn right onto rue de la Prairie beside house No. 5	GR sign	NW
19	180	Continue straight ahead on rue Bas des Prés		SW
20	300	Keep right on the track		SW
21	200	Continue straight ahead following cycle track no. 6	GR sign	SW
22	700	Turn left remaining on the track		SE
23	400	Turn right towards a mini-roundabout and cross straight over on rue des Trois Ponts direction Bessines	GR sign	S
24	1200	Turn left into a wooded area	GR sign	SE
25	90	Cross the narrow Japanese style bridge	GR sign	S
26	110	At the T-junction turn left beside the Gîtes d'Etape		SE
27	90	At the T-junction in the centre of Bessines, turn left	GR sign	E
28	100	Turn right on rue de l'Eglise, with the Mairie directly on your right	GR sign	S
29	80	Turn left onto a path, chemin Piétonnier	GR sign	SE
30	200	Turn left towards the mini-roundabout and take the first exit on rue du Logis	GR sign	SW

Niort to Beauvoir-sur-Niort 33.7km

Way Point	Distance	Directions	Verification Point	Compass
31	190	Turn right on chemin du Moulin	GR sign	NW
32	100	Continue straight ahead on a gravel path	GR sign	W
33	400	At the crossroads go straight ahead remaining on chemin du Moulin	GR sign	SW
34	800	Cross over the minor road to continue on the track	GR sign	W
35	400	At the junction at the end of rue de la Garenne turn left on rue Jean Richard	GR sign	S
36	500	Continue straight ahead towards the main road	GR sign	S
37	180	Cross the main road (D3) onto an unmade track	GR sign	S
38	1200	At a T-junction in the tracks turn left	GR sign	SE
39	1000	At a T-junction with a major road (D611) turn right. **Note:-** this is a very busy road, but horses can gain some protection by taking the verge behind the crash barrier	GR sign	S
40	300	Turn left off the main road direction Chantigné		E
41	300	Turn right onto an unmade track, parallel to the main road	GR sign	S
42	800	Bear right on the main track		SW
43	400	Continue straight ahead and parallel to the main road	GR sign	SW
44	700	At a T-junction turn left direction Fontenay	GR sign	S
45	400	Turn left onto rue des Chambeaux	GR sign	SE
46	80	At the junction continue straight ahead on rue des Chambeaux		SE
47	600	At a T-junction turn left	GR sign	E
48	1100	Remain on the road as it turns to the right	GR sign	S
49	400	At the crossroads go straight ahead towards the top of the hill		S

Niort to Beauvoir-sur-Niort 33.7km

Niort to Beauvoir-sur-Niort 33.7km

Way Point	Distance	Directions	Verification Point	Compass
50	190	At the crossroads turn left, a large pylon on your right	GR sign	SE
51	800	At the end of the track, pass through the break in the hedge and cross the busy road		SE
52	40	Continue at right angles to the road on a gravelled track towards trees on the horizon		SE
53	400	At T-junction with a minor road turn right towards the village of Bassée		S
54	400	At the junction continue straight ahead on rue de Belair avoiding the GR sign to the left. This leads to an unnecessary dog-leg around the village		SW
55	400	At the crossroads in Bassée turn right on rue de Blanchaux	GR sign	W
56	400	Turn left on the D102 direction Granzay	GR sign	S
57	500	Just after crossing the bridge bear right direction Blaise	GR sign	SW
58	500	Turn left on rue du Chêne Saint Loius	GR sign	S
59	160	At a T-junction turn right onto route de Blaise direction Pouvreau	GR sign	W
60	300	Continue straight ahead ignoring the GR dog-leg to the right		W
61	300	At T-junction turn left onto rue de Pouvreau	GR sign	S
62	800	At junction with a minor road bear right and then immediately left to leave the road on the unmade track	GR sign	S
63	300	Continue straight ahead on the track		S
64	200	Keep right on the track		S
65	200	At a T-junction with a minor road turn left, away from the village of Allerit	GR sign	S
66	400	At a T-junction turn left	GR sign	SE

Way Point	Distance	Directions	Verification Point	Compass
67	1800	At a crossroads continue straight ahead	GR sign	SE
68	1200	At a crossroads continue straight ahead on rue de l'Ecole into the village of Limouillas	GR sign	SE
69	300	At a T-junction turn left onto route de Château d'Eau	GR sign	NE
70	130	Turn right onto an unmade track opposite rue des Gîtes	GR sign	SE
71	800	At a T-junction in the tracks turn left with the autoroute directly on the right	GR sign	NE
72	200	At the T-junction with a minor road turn right and cross over the road bridge		SE
73	700	At a crossroads go straight ahead	GR sign	SE
74	200	Turn right into the village of le Cormenier	GR sign	S
75	90	Continue straight ahead		S
76	300	Turn left onto chemin Neuf		E
77	170	Turn right onto rue de la Vignes		S
78	300	At a crossroads continue straight ahead on rue de la Vignes		S
79	300	Turn left down a narrow alley towards the main road		E
80	110	Arrive at the square in the centre of Beauvoir-sur-Niort		

Niort to Beauvoir-sur-Niort 33.7km

Niort to Beauvoir-sur-Niort 33.7km

Accommodation - Hotel / B&B	Price	Opening	Animals
Reix Hôtel, rte La Rochelle 79000 BESSINES Tel: 0033 (0)5 49 09 15 15	B2	All Year	🐴
Espace Hôtel, rte La Rochelle 79000 BESSINES Tel: 0033 (0)5 49 09 08 07	B2	All Year	🐴
Calmel Jean-Pierre, Clairias 79270 FRONTENAY ROHAN ROHAN Tel: 0033 (0)5 49 04 58 42	B2	All Year	🐴
BERTHOME Lucie et Frédéric, 14a Chemin du Marais Lieu-dit Faugerit 79270 FRONTENAY ROHAN-ROHAN Tel: 0033 (0)5 49 77 55 51	B3	All Year	🐴
Auberge du Cheval Blanc, 23 pl Champ de Foire 79170 BRIOUX SUR BOUTONNE Tel: 0033 (0)5 49 07 52 08 **Note:** 1.2km from Beauvoir-sur-Niort	B2	All Year	🐴
Richard Marie-Claire, 463 r Ecoles, CORMENIER (LE) 79360 BEAUVOIR-SUR-NIORT Tel: 0033 (0)5 49 09 70 42	B2	All Year	🐴

Camping	Price	Opening	Animals
Camping Municipal, av Marais Poitevin 79460 MAGNE Tel: 0033 (0)5 49 35 71 81 **Note:** 2km from Bessines	B1	All Year	🐴

Equestrian Centre

Maison du Cheval, Port Jaguin La Garette 79270 SANSAIS
Tel: 0033 (0)5 49 35 35 35 **Note:** 4km from Frontenay-Rohan-Rohan

Useful Contacts

Doctor

Véron Nicolas, 246 av St Jean 79360 BEAUVOIR SUR NIORT
Tel: 0033 (0)5 49 09 70 43

Veterinary

Coulibaly Moussa, 280 av St Jean 79360 BEAUVOIR SUR NIORT
Tel: 0033 (0)5 49 04 61 09 Mobile: 0033 (0)6 24 82 47 83

Farrier

Laurent Alain, 2 r Puits Gros Bois 79370 PRAILLES Tel: 0033 (0)5 49 32 91 98

Known in Latin as Aunedonacum, **Aulnay-de-Saintonge's** history begins in Roman times, when it was a small town along the road between the prominent ancient cities of Poitiers and Saintes. In the Middle Ages, the road continued to be used, especially as part of the pilgrimage route from Paris to Santiago de Compostela. The first known church in Aulnay-de-Saintonge (of unknown date) was called St-Pierre-de-la-Tour, which was given to the Benedictine monks of St-Cyprien Abbey in Poitiers in the 11th century. In the early 12th century, the church was transferred to the chapter of Poitiers Cathedral. Shortly thereafter it was rebuilt, most likely under the direction of Poitiers' canons, in about 1140 to 1170. The Eglise Saint-Pierre stands at the west end of Aulnay-de-Saintonge. Most visitors approach the church from the east, which provides the loveliest view of the church. The cream-colored stone is accentuated by the deep green of several cypress trees in the churchyard, whose pointed shape also echoes the church spire. Both the tall spire and upper section of the tower are Gothic, dating from the late 13th or early 14th century. Moving around to the south side, one of the most magnificent aspects of the church comes into

view: the south portal. There is no tympanum, but the four archivolts are alive with sculpture. The west facade is another fine example of Romanesque art, although it has suffered a great deal of damage. The upper half was once richly decorated, including an equestrian sculpture of Constantine or Charlemagne, but none of this has survived; it was sadly replaced with the

present plain facade in the 15th century, as part of essential repair work. The twin conical turrets on the ends are original from the 12th century. The interior of the church is simple and almost austere: a tall nave with a pointed vault and side aisles, a transept, and small choir with east apse. The transept crossing is topped with a cupola with an unusual design of eight radiating ribs, resting on pendatives. The pillars of the nave are quite sizeable, allowing for large sculptures on the capitals. These depict a variety of human masks, creatures, biblical scenes and foliage. Near the door in the south aisle is a capital with three elephants - drawn, as usual in this period, a bit inaccurately. A helpful Latin inscription explains: "Here are elephants." Also in the south aisle are twin male masks (a similar one nearby was left unfinished) and Delilah cutting Samson's hair as he sleeps.

Beauvoir-sur-Niort to Aulnay-de-Staintonge 32.9km

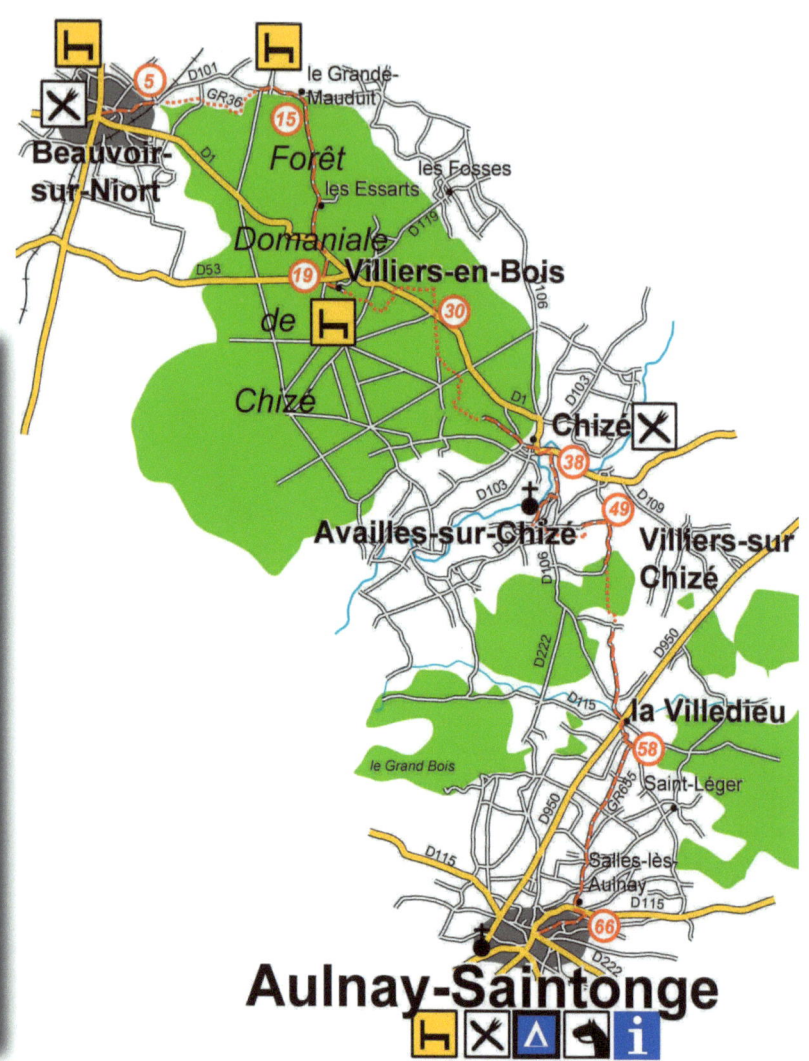

Route Summary: another long section but rewarded by reaching the GR655 - Voie de Tours. The route traverses the huge Forêt de Chizé and then follows minor roads and broad tracks before joining the GR655 in the village of la Villedieu. We have eliminated the largest of the meanders taken by the GR36, but examination of the map will show other possibilities for further reducing the length of the section for those willing to make more use of the highways.

Way Point	Distance	Directions	Verification Point	Compass
1		From the traffic lights beside the square in the centre of Beauvoir-sur-Niort bear left across the square. **Note**:- we will avoid the GR36 for the first 1.5km in order to take the quieter D101 and reduce the overall distance		NE
2	80	Turn right on the D101 direction Marigny		E
3	200	At the mini-roundabout take the first exit direction Marigny		E
4	100	Bear left on the D101		E
5	1200	Just after the level crossing bear right onto an unmade track – do not take the track to the right	GR sign	E
6	300	Bear left on the track	GR sign	E
7	700	At the junction with a minor road turn right on the road		S
8	60	Turn left off the road onto a grass track in the trees	GR sign	E
9	300	Continue straight ahead on the grass track	GR sign	E
10	600	At a junction with a broad gravel track turn left	GR sign	NE
11	700	At a junction with a minor road turn right keeping the trees directly to your right	GR sign	E
12	160	Continue straight ahead	GR sign	E
13	800	In the village of le Grand Mauduit continue straight ahead on route de la Forêt		SE
14	170	Turn right onto route des Essarts		SE
15	90	Continue straight ahead on the long straight forest road – route Forestière N° 13 - route des Essarts. **Note**:- the GR36 turns left at this point following a tortuous route around the forest and adding considerable distance to the route. We will rejoin the GR at Way Point #22		S
16	2300	Continue straight ahead on route Forestière des Alleuds	The hamlet of les Essarts to the left	S

Beauvoir-sur-Niort to Aulnay-de-Saintonge 32.9km

Way Point	Distance	Directions	Verification Point	Compass
17	900	Turn left on the D1 direction Chizé		SE
18	400	Turn right on the road direction Villiers-en-Bois		S
19	500	At the crossroads continue straight ahead in the direction of le Bourg	*Chemin du Prioulet*	SE
20	120	Bear right on the road		SE
21	130	Bear right onto chemin de la Forêt	GR sign and Gîte d'Etape	E
22	1000	Beside a wooden gate turn right towards the road keeping the wild-life park – Zoodyssée -immediately on the right	GR sign	S
23	50	Continue straight ahead beside the park offices	GR sign	SW
24	70	Bear left through the green and white barrier		E
25	60	Turn right on the track following the sign for Forêt Domaniale de Chizé	Pass small concrete building on the left	S
26	40	Turn left into the forest leaving a large white building on the right	GR sign	E
27	500	At a fork in the track, bear left	GR sign	NE
28	300	Cross straight over the road and bear right on the less major track at an oblique angle to the road	GR sign	E
29	800	At a T-junction in the tracks turn right on the broad track		S
30	500	The track returns to the road, cross over continuing straight ahead	GR sign	S
31	1800	Just after rounding the corner turn right into the woods on a narrow track N° 164 on the left and N° 166 on the right	GR sign	S
32	70	At a fork in the track, bear right	GR sign	S
33	120	At a fork in the track, bear left	GR sign	S
34	140	At a fork in the track, bear left	GR sign	S
35	400	At the junction with the broader track turn left	GR sign	SE

Beauvoir-sur-Niort to Aulnay-de-Saintonge 32.9km

Way Point	Distance	Directions	Verification Point	Compass
36	1600	At the road junction bear right into Chizé on rue de l'Hôtel de Ville		SE
37	500	Take the right fork on the D1 route des Ponts	GR sign	E
38	400	Turn right on the D106 direction la Villedieu	GR sign	S
39	900	Take the right fork onto a smaller road	GR sign	S
40	120	Turn right in the direction of l'Abbaye	GR sign	SW
41	800	Turn right onto rue du Lavoir	GR sign	SW
42	110	Turn left with the church to your right, remaining on rue du Lavoir	GR sign	S
43	50	At a T-junction turn left	Beside house N° 41	E
44	200	Take the right fork		SE
45	160	At a crossroads, go straight ahead and then onto a pathway with the cemetery directly on the left, passing a calvaire on the right	GR sign	E
46	700	At the junction with the broader track bear left		E
47	190	At a T-junction in the tracks turn left with a line of trees to your left		NW
48	200	At a junction with a minor road turn right keeping between 2 rows of trees	GR sign	E
49	600	At a crossroads turn right	GR sign	S
50	1000	Bear left onto an unmade track	GR sign	S
51	1200	Turn right keeping a row of trees on your right		S
52	200	At the crossroads go straight head beside house N° 21 - Buffageasse. **Note**:- this is the point at which we leave the GR36 for the last time	GR sign	S
53	1800	At the junction with the D115e2 turn left on the road towards the village of la Villedieu		SE

Beauvoir-sur-Niort to Aulnay-de-Saintonge 32.9km

Way Point	Distance	Directions	Verification Point	Compass
54	400	At the crossroads with the busy D950 in the centre of la Villedieu turn right on the main road – direction Aulnay. **Note:-** we have now joined the GR 655 – la voie de Tours or via Turonensis which Santiago pilgrims will follow to Ostabat	GR sign	SW
55	130	Turn left onto chemin de la Procession with the church on your right	GR sign	SE
56	200	Turn right on chemin de Compostelle	GR sign	SW
57	130	Turn left beside the cockle shell sign		SE
58	180	Turn right following the cockle shell		SW
59	800	Continue straight ahead following cockle shell		SW
60	800	At a crossroads continue straight ahead	Cockle shell	S
61	1000	At a T-junction turn left and then immediately right up the hill		S
62	300	At a crossroads continue straight ahead		S
63	500	Bear right on the D222e1 down the hill towards Salles-lès-Aulnay		SW
64	130	Continue straight ahead down the hill		S
65	400	At the crossroads in Salles-lès-Aulnay turn left on the D129, beside house N° 27	GR sign	E
66	300	Turn right	Cockle shell	SW
67	300	Turn right onto an unmade road	Cockle shell	W
68	900	Turn right on rue de l'Abreuvoir	GR sign	NW
69	100	Arrive in Aulnay-de-Saintonge centre at the junction of rue de l'Abreuvoir and rue de la Cour à Madame	Place Aristide Briand to the left	

Beauvoir-sur-Niort to Aulnay-de-Saintonge 32.9km

Accommodation - Hotel/B&B	Price	Opening	Animals
Garnaud Jean, 10 rte Forêt 79360 MARIGNY Tel: 0033 (0)5 49 09 72 20	B2	All Year	🐴
Le Relais D'Aulnay, 14 rte Cognac 17470 AULNAY-DE-SAINTONGE Tel: 0033 (0)5 46 33 16 77	B2	All Year	🐴
Hôtel du Donjon, 4 r Hivers 17470 AULNAY-DE-SAINTONGE Tel: 0033 (0)5 46 33 67 67	B3	All Year	🐴

Religious Accommodation	Price	Opening	Animals
Curé Emmanuel Oré 4, Cour à Madame 17470 AULNAY-DE-SAINTONGE Tel: 0033 (0)5 46 33 10 49	Donation	All Year	🐴

Hostel	Price	Opening	Animals
COMMUNE DE VILLIERS EN BOIS 79360 VILLIERS EN BOIS Tel: 0033 (0)5 49 76 79 67	B1	All Year	🐴

Camping	Price	Opening	Animals
Camping Muncipal, rue des Merlonges 17470 AULNAY-DE-SAINTONGE Tel: 0033 (0)5 49 07 46 (Mairie)	B1	All Year	🐴

Equestrian Centre

Lafargue Michel, Le Riveau 17470 AULNAY   Tel: 0033 (0)5 46 26 32 38

Useful Contacts

Tourist Offices

OFFICE DE TOURISME du Canton d'Aulnay de Saintonge, 290, Av de l'Eglise, 17470 AULNAY-DE-SAINTONGE   Tel: 0033 (0)5 46 33 14 44   otaulnay@free.fr
http://tourisme.aulnay.info

Doctor

Hubert Guy, 1 chem Loubie 17470 AULNAY-DE-SAINTONGE
Tel: 0033 (0)5 46 33 12 19

Veterinary

Caron Christelle, 23 r Carmes 17470 AULNAY-DE-SAINTONGE
Tel: 0033 (0)5 46 33 10 33

Farrier

Lesueur Bruno, 10 r Place Vinageville 17490 BRESDON   Tel: 0033 (0)5 46 26 67 26

Aulnay to Saint-Jean-d'Angely 25km

Route Summary: the final section is well marked on largely broad farm tracks and makes for easy going for all groups despite adopting a winding course over the last few kilometres before reaching Saint-Jean-d'Angely

Way Point	Distance	Directions	Verification Point	Compass
1		From the junction of rue de l'Abreuvoir and rue de la Cour à Madame beside the place Aristide Briand continue on the small road rue de Beaulieu	GR sign	NW
2	80	At the T-junction turn left	GR sign	W
3	60	Keep right on rue des Carmes	GR sign	W
4	700	At the T-junction with the busy D950 turn left remaining on the left side of the road. **Note:-** to avoid the busy road it is possible to cross the church yard and turn left on the far side	Skirting the church of Saint Pierre de la Tour, Saint Jacques sign on the right side of the road	SW
5	60	Turn left onto rue Basse de l'Eglise keeping the church immediately to your left		SE
6	500	Turn right onto rue des Portes	GR sign	SE
7	200	At the T-junction turn right on rue de la Porte Saint-Jean	GR sign	SW
8	170	Go straight ahead on the D121 direction Cherbonnières	GR sign	SW
9	100	Turn right on the D129 – route des Pèlerins – direction Varaize	Cockle shell	SW
10	140	Turn left just beyond the industrial building on your right	Cockle shell	S
11	500	Continue straight ahead through the wooden barriers and up the hill		S
12	1500	At the T-junction with a minor road turn right	Cockle shell	W
13	900	At the T-junction turn right	Cockle shell	NW
14	500	At the crossroads continue straight ahead into the village of Brie	Cockle shell	W
15	300	In the village take the left fork down the hill onto rue du Ruisseau	Cockle shell and GR sign	S
16	200	At the T-junction turn right onto rue de Brie	Cockle shell	W
17	300	Bear left off the road onto a track	Cockle shell	S

Aulnay to Saint-Jean-d'Angely 25km

Way Point	Distance	Directions	Verification Point	Compass
18	600	At the T-junction with a minor road turn right	Cockle shell	W
19	700	At the T-junction turn left up the hill	Cockle shell	S
20	800	At the crossroads continue straight ahead on rue de la Garenne	GR sign	SW
21	130	Turn left	Cockle shell – Saint-Jean-d'Angely 17km	S
22	900	At the T-junction turn right onto a gravel track	Cockle shell	SW
23	800	At the T-junction turn right	Cockle shell	W
24	500	At the crossroads continue straight ahead	Cockle shell	SW
25	900	At the T-junction with a minor road turn right	Cockle shell	W
26	600	At the crossroads in les Eglises-d'Argenteuil turn right on rue Saint-Vivien	Cockle shell	N
27	170	At the junction with the D950 turn left towards the centre of the village		SW
28	60	Turn right on rue des Métairies	GR sign	W
29	600	Bear right onto the main road – D127el	Cockle shell	W
30	600	Bear right into the village of Vervant		NW
31	700	Turn left on rue de la Boutonne	GR sign	SW
32	300	Take the left fork with the Salle des Fêtes immediately to your left	GR sign	S
33	190	Take the right fork	Cockle shell – Saint-Jean-d'Angely 10km	S
34	1600	At the T-junction turn right on rue de Vervant	Cockle shell	SW
35	300	At the T-junction turn right on rue des Grands Champs into Poursay-Garnaud	GR sign	W
36	90	Turn left on rue de l'Eglise	Cockle shell	SW
37	160	Bear left with the church on your left		SW
38	50	Take the right fork onto rue de l'Ecole	GR sign	SW
39	400	At the T-junction turn right with the Mairie directly on the right		W
40	500	Bear right on rue de la Sablière	GR sign	SW

Aulnay to Saint-Jean-d'Angely 25km

Way Point	Distance	Directions	Verification Point	Compass
40	500	Bear right on rue de la Sablière	GR sign	SW
41	150	Turn right onto rue du Moulin and cross the bridge		NW
42	700	At the T-junction in Courcelles turn left on rue du Bourg		SW
43	400	Turn left onto chemin de Grenet	Cockle shell	W
44	1600	At the T-junction turn left	GR sign	W
45	300	Turn left and left again following the road and the sign for Gens du Voyage	Cockle shell	S
46	1200	Turn right onto an unmade track	Cockle shell	W
47	1200	At a mini-roundabout turn right onto rue de la Sacristinerie	GR sign	N
48	300	At the T-junction turn left towards a level-crossing		SW
49	200	At the crossroads continue straight ahead on allée d'Aussy	GR sign	SW
50	500	At the traffic lights turn right in the direction of Centre Ville	GR sign	NW
51	90	At the crossroads continue straight ahead on rue Pascal Bourcy towards Centre Ville	GR sign	NW
52	120	Turn right onto rue de la Grosse Horloge and then immediately follow the road to the left to pass under the clock-tower		NW
53	160	Bear right into place du Pilori and proceed towards the elaborate well le Puits du Pilori	Tourist Office to the left	NW
54	70	Bear left on rue de l'Abbaye		W
55	150	Arrive at the entrance to the Abbey in the centre of Saint-Jean-d'Angely. **Note:** just 921 km to Santiago		

Aulnay to Saint-Jean-d'Angely 25km

Accommodation - Hotel/B&B	Price	Opening	Animals
Bordessoules Jean Louis, 3 r Regnaud 17400 SAINT JEAN D'ANGELY Tel: 0033 (0)9 60 03 48 55	B2	All Year	
Marit Pascale, 23 r Verdun 17400 SAINT JEAN D'ANGELY Tel: 0033 (0)5 46 32 19 66 pascale.marit@laposte.net	B2	All Year	
Hôtel Restaurant de la Place, pl Hôtel de Ville 17400 SAINT JEAN D'ANGELY Tel: 0033 (0)5 46 32 69 11	B2	All Year	
Hôtel du Jardin Public, 35 av Gén Leclerc 17400 SAINT JEAN D'ANGELY Tel: 0033 (0)5 46 32 13 12	B2	All Year	
Hôtel Sweet Hôtel, 25 Place du Marché 17400 SAINT JEAN D'ANGÉLY Mobile: 0033 (0)6 16 68 50 79	B3	All Year	
Hôtel Restaurant La Goulebenèze, 21 av Port Mahon 17400 SAINT JEAN D'ANGÉLY Tel: 0033 (0)5 46 32 57 67	B2	All Year	
Hôtel La Paix, 6 all.D'Aussy 17400 SAINT JEAN D'ANGÉLY Tel: 0033 (0)5 46 32 00 93	B2	All Year	

Religious/Pilgrim Accommodation	Price	Opening	Animals
Centre de Culture Européene, Abbaye Royal 17400 ST JEAN D'ANGELY Tel: 0033 (0)5 46 32 04 72 www.ccangely.org	B1	All Year	
Gair Catherine, 36 av Rochefort 17400 SAINT JEAN D'ANGELY Tel: 0033 (0)5 46 26 17 91 gair@9online.fr	B1	All Year	

Camping	Price	Opening	Animals
Camping Val de Boutonne, 56 quai Bernouet 17400 SAINT JEAN D'ANGELY Tel: 0033 (0)5 46 32 26 16	B1	All Year	

Equestrian Centre			
Centre Hippique de Mazeray, 11 rte Ste Même 17400 MAZERAY Tel: 0033 (0)5 46 59 16 54 **Note:** 5.21km from St Jean d'Angely			

Aulnay to Saint-Jean-d'Angely 25km

Useful Contacts

Tourist Offices

Office de tourisme St Jean d'Angely et St Hilaire de Villefranche, BP 117 8 r grosse Horloge 17416 SAINT JEAN D'ANGÉLY Tel: 0033 (0)5 46 32 04 72 office.tourisme@angely.net

Doctor

Plasseraud-Desgranges Jean-Claude, 4 pl André Lemoyne 17400 SAINT JEAN D'ANGELY Tel: 0033 (0)5 46 59 05 64

Veterinary

Charpiat Yves Debray Louison, 2 r Louis Audouin Dubreuil 17400 SAINT JEAN D'ANGELY   Tel: 0033 (0)5 46 59 05 25

Farrier

Rey Raphael, 24 r Aristide Briand 17100 SAINTES   Mobile: 0033 (0)6 30 28 11 77

Founded in the ninth century to house a relic of Saint John the Baptist (his cranium) and rebuilt in the 14th, 17th and 18th centuries because of repeated destruction the Abbey is now a listed building. It remains the most remarkable piece of architecture of **Saint-Jean d'Angély**, a town which has kept its medieval charm. Situated on the pilgrim route leading pilgrims to Santiago de Compostela, the edifice still constitutes a major stopping-off point. Since 1989, the Royal Abbey has housed the Centre of European Culture, which has breathed new life into the Abbey by restoring it as a historical and cultural site. From 1989 to 1997, the restoration of the monastic buildings has been carried out according to the needs of the Centre of European Culture, with an emphasis placed on accommodation, as well as rooms for conferences, reunions and workshops.

The culmination of the siege of Saint-Jean-d'Angély: the inhabitants open the gates to Jean II of France, August 1351

The list below gives details of the churches and religious organisations either in or near towns along the route. These have not specifically stated that accommodation is provided for pilgrims, but it is likely that a phone call will put you in contact with someone who will be able/willing to help.

ST JAMES	Presbytère, 5 r Presbytère 50240 SAINT JAMES Tel/ 0033 (0)2 33 48 31 40
FOUGERES	Gratien Louis, 11 Bis r Lesueur 35300 FOUGERES Tel: 0033 (0)2 99 99 35 59
	Presbytère Saint Léonard, sacristie, r Nationale 35300 FOUGERES Tel: 0033 (0)2 99 94 96 19
	Presbytère de Bonabry, r Abbé Joly 35300 FOUGERES Tel: 0033 (0)2 99 99 05 38
VITRE	Presbytère Saint Martin, 36 r Paris 35500 VITRE Tel: 0033 (0)2 99 75 02 78
	Communauté des Religieuses, La Guilmarais 35500 VITRE Tel: 0033 (0)2 99 75 39 50
GUERCHE DE BRETAGNE (LA)	Presbytère, 25 r Neuve 35130 GUERCHE DE BRETAGNE (LA) Tel: 0033 (0)2 99 96 22 10
POUANCE	Presbytère, 1 pl Madeleine 49420 POUANCE Tel: 0033 (0)2 41 92 41 40
LION D'ANGERS (LE)	Paroisse Saint Martin, r Anselme Bouvet 49220 LION D'ANGERS (LE) Tel:0033 (0)2 41 95 31 02
ANGERS	Presbytère de la Cathédrale, 4 r St Christophe 49100 ANGERS Tel: 0033 (0)2 41 87 58 45
	Centre Saint Maurice, 2 r Oisellerie 49100 ANGERS Tel:0033 (0)2 41 88 46 94
	Presbytère Saint Laud, 4 r Marceau 49100 ANGERS Tel: 0033 (0)2 41 87 60 56
	Communauté Filles Charité du Sacré Coeur Blancheraie, 4 r Esvière 49100 ANGERS Tel: 0033 (0)2 41 87 52 56
	Presbytère Saint Joseph, 2 r St Joseph 49100 ANGERS Tel: 0033 (0)2 41 19 95 70
	Presbytère Saint Serge, 2 r Emile Hatais 49100 ANGERS Tel: 0033 (0)2 41 43 66 76
	Presbytère de Sainte Bernadette, 9 r Locarno 49100 ANGERS Tel: 0033 (0)2 41 66 62 01
	Presbytère de Saint Antoine, 10 r Béranger 49100 ANGERS Tel: 0033 (0)2 41 43 76 33
	Presbytère Saint Martin des Champs, 14 bd Abbé Edouard Chauvat 49000 ANGERS Tel: 0033 (0)2 41 66 90 47
	Presbytère Sainte Marie de Belle Beille, 3 r Eugénie Mansion 49000 ANGERS Tel: 0033 (0)2 41 48 23 51
	Presbytère de Saint Léonard, 359 r St Léonard 49000 ANGERS Tel: 0033 (0)2 41 66 90 90
	Presbytère Saint Jean, r Ecriture 49100 ANGERS Tel: 0033 (0)2 41 43 92 87

PONTS DE CE (LES)	Presbytère Saint Maurille, 78 r Commdt Bourgeois 49130 PONTS DE CE (LES)	Tel: 0033 (0)2 41 44 60 81
MONTREUIL BELLAY	Presbytère, 40 r Ermites 49260 MONTREUIL BELLAY	Tel: 0033 (0)2 41 40 31 10
THOUARS	Cure, 11 pl St Médard 79100 THOUARS	Tel: 0033 (0)5 49 66 26 98
AIRVAULT	Cure, 3 r Gendarmerie 79600 AIRVAULT	Tel: 0033 (0)5 49 64 71 74
PARTHENAY	Cure Saint Laurent, 1 pl St Laurent 79200 PARTHENAY	Tel: 0033 (0)5 49 64 05 40
NIORT	Cure de Souché, 6 r Sableau 79000 NIORT	Tel: 0033 (0)5 49 24 06 60
	Cure Saint Etienne, 50 r Gambetta 79000 NIORT	Tel: 0033 (0)5 49 79 22 68
	Cure Saint Florent, 1 r Camille Desmoulins 79000 NIORT	Tel: 0033 (0)5 49 79 22 28
	Cure Saint Hilaire, 34 r 14 Juillet 79000 NIORT	Tel: 0033 (0)5 49 24 08 89
	Cure de Saint Liguaire, 3 imp Abbaye 79000 NIORT	Tel: 0033 (0)5 49 73 97 51
AULNAY-DE-SAINTONGE	Paroisse Notre Dame de Saintonge, 4 r Cour à Madame 17470 AULNAY	Tel: 0033 (0)5 46 33 10 49
SAINT JEAN D'ANGELY	Assoc Diocésaine De La Rochelle Saintes, 4 r Maréchaux 17400 SAINT JEAN D'ANGELY	Tel: 0033 (0)5 46 59 01 24

Section No.	Section Name	Distance	Distance in Km	Scale	Map Reference no.	Title
1	Le Mont Saint Michel to Saint James	22160	22.2	1:25,000	1215ET	IGN Top 25, AVRANCHES/GRANVILLE/LE MONT-SAINT-MICHEL
2	Saint James to Montours	12980	12.0	1:25,000	1316O	IGN Top 25, SAINT-JAMES
				1:25,000	1316O	IGN Top 25, SAINT-JAMES
3	Montours to Fougères	18710	18.7	1:25,000	1316O	IGN Top 25, SAINT-JAMES
				1:25,000	1317E	IGN Top 25, FOUGERES
4	Fougères to Châtillon-en-Vendelais	20090	20.1	1:25,000	1317E	IGN Top 25, FOUGERES
5	Châtillon-en-Vendelais to Vitré	16400	16.4	1:25,000	1318E	IGN Top 25, VITRE
6	Vitré to la Guerche-de-Bretagne	26470	26.5	1:25,000	1318E	IGN Top 25, VITRE
				1:25,000	1319E	IGN Top 25, LA GUERCHE-DE-BRETAGNE
7	La Guerche-de-Bretagne to Pouancé	32120	32.1	1:25,000	1319E	IGN Top 25, LA GUERCHE-DE-BRETAGNE
				1:25,000	1320E	IGN Top 25, POUANCE
8	Pouancé to Segré	38800	38.8	1:25,000	1320E	IGN Top 25, POUANCE
				1:25,000	1420O	IGN Top 25, CRAON
				1:25,000	1421E	IGN Top 25, SEGRE
9	Segré to le-Lion-d'Angers	21500	21.5	1:25,000	1421E	IGN Top 25, SEGRE
				1:25,000	1521O	IGN Top 25, LE LION-D'ANGERS
10	Le-Lion-d'Angers to Angers	28640	28.6	1:25,000	1521O	IGN Top 25, LE LION-D'ANGERS

Section No.	Section Name	Distance	Distance in Km	Map		
				Scale	Reference no.	Title
11	Angers to Brissac-Quincé	26590	26.6	1:25,000	1522O	IGN Top 25, ANGERS
				1:25,000	1522O	IGN Top 25, ANGERS
				1:25,000	1622O	IGN Top 25, MAZE
12	Brissac-Quincé to Rochemenier	24510	24.5	1:25,000	1622O	IGN Top 25, MAZE
				1:25,000	1523E	IGN Top 25, THOUARCE
				1:25,000	1623O	IGN Top 25, DOUE-LA-FONTAINE
13	Rochemenier to Montreuil-Bellay	21350	21.4	1:25,000	1623O	IGN Top 25, DOUE-LA-FONTAINE
				1:25,000	1624E	IGN Top 25,MONTREIL-BELLAY
14	Montreuil-Bellay to Thouars	32810	32.8	1:25,000	1624E	IGN Top 25,MONTREIL-BELLAY
				1:25,000	1624O	IGN Top 25,THOUARS-NORD/LE-PUY-NORTE-DAME
15	Thouars to Airvault	29000	29.0	1:25,000	1625O	IGN Top 25,THOUARS
				1:25,000	1625E	IGN Top 25,AIRVAULT
16	Airvault to Parthenay	30910	30.9	1:25,000	1625E	IGN Top 25,AIRVAULT
				1:25,000	1626E	IGN Top 25,THENEZAY
				1:25,000	1626O	IGN Top 25,PARTHENAY

Section No.	Section Name	Distance	Distance in Km	Scale	Map Reference no.	Title
17	Parthenay to Champdeniers-Saint-Denis	28000	28.0	1:25,000	1626O	IGN Top 25,PARTHENAY
				1:25,000	1627O	IGN Top 25,MAZIERES-EN-GÂTINE
				1:25,000	1527E	IGN Top 25,SECONDIGNY
18	Champdeniers-Saint-Denis to Niort	24790	24.8	1:25,000	1527E	IGN Top 25,SECONDIGNY
				1:25,000	1528E	IGN Top 25,NIORT
19	Niort to Beauvoir-sur-Niort	33660	33.7	1:25,000	1528E	IGN Top 25,NIORT
				1:25,000	1529E	IGN Top 25,FONTENAY-ROHAN/FÔRET-DE-CHIZE
20	Beauvoir-sur-Niort to Aulnay-Saintonge	32960	32.0	1:25,000	1529E	IGN Top 25,FONTENAY-ROHAN/FÔRET-DE-CHIZE
				1:25,000	1529O	IGN Top 25,BRIOUS-SUR-BOUTONNE
				1:25,000	1530O	IGN Top 25,AULNAY
21	Aulnay-Saintonge to Saint-Jean-d'Angely	25000	25.0	1:25,000	1530O	IGN Top 25,AULNAY
				1:25,000	1530E	IGN Top 25,SAINT-JEAN-D'ANGELY
	Total	547450	547.4			

The longest journey begins with a single step
Lao Tzu

Name:
Address:

Date Started:
Place Started:
Date Ended:
Signature:
Horse:
Bicycle:
On Foot:

Pilgrim record - Signature & Stamp

Pilgrim record - Signature & Stamp

Pilgrim record - Signature & Stamp

Pilgrim record - Signature & Stamp

Pilgrim record - Signature & Stamp	Pilgrim record - Signature & Stamp
Pilgrim record - Signature & Stamp	Pilgrim record - Signature & Stamp
Pilgrim record - Signature & Stamp	Pilgrim record - Signature & Stamp
Pilgrim record - Signature & Stamp	Pilgrim record - Signature & Stamp

Pilgrim record - Signature & Stamp	Pilgrim record - Signature & Stamp
Pilgrim record - Signature & Stamp	Pilgrim record - Signature & Stamp
Pilgrim record - Signature & Stamp	Pilgrim record - Signature & Stamp
Pilgrim record - Signature & Stamp	Pilgrim record - Signature & Stamp

Pilgrim record - Signature & Stamp	Pilgrim record - Signature & Stamp
Pilgrim record - Signature & Stamp	Pilgrim record - Signature & Stamp
Pilgrim record - Signature & Stamp	Pilgrim record - Signature & Stamp
Pilgrim record - Signature & Stamp	Pilgrim record - Signature & Stamp

www.ingramcontent.com/pod-product-compliance
Lightning Source LLC
Chambersburg PA
CBHW042308150426
43198CB00001B/2